MW00666985

NATURE SCHOOL
THE WORKBOOK

100+ Activities, Games, and Puzzles

Lauren Giordano
Stephanie Hathaway
Laura Stroup

QUARRY

CONTENTS

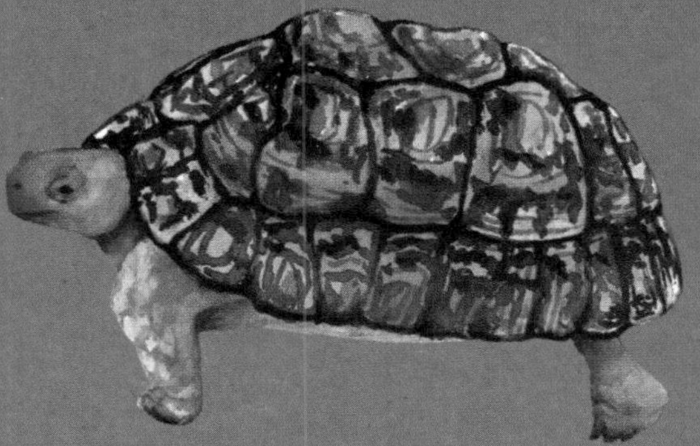

INTRODUCTION

Welcome to *Nature School: The Workbook*, and thank you for joining us on this learning adventure. This workbook is filled with information, activities, and exploration inspiration to help you discover and appreciate the natural world both near and far. You will study five different biomes from around the globe, reviewing key information about living and nonliving things and their interactions within ecosystems. You will have the opportunity to answer questions, create a nature journal, label diagrams, draw and paint, and do experiments, plus much more.

We encourage you to pair this workbook with *Nature School: Lessons and Activities to Inspire Children's Love for Everything Wild* to maximize your educational experience. However you choose to explore, it's our hope that you make lasting connections with nature and share what you learn with others.

1

TEMPERATE FORESTS

Discover!

DISCOVER!

In an **ecosystem**, living things interact with each other and the nonliving things in the environment around them. Living things such as plants, animals, fungi, and microbes are known as biotic factors. Nonliving things, also called abiotic factors, include soil, water, rocks, and sunlight, among others. Biotic and abiotic factors often build connections through food chains, where one living thing eats another, creating a flow of nutrients and energy from plants growing in soil with sunlight and water to large predators that feed on smaller animals.

Temperate forest ecosystems are found in parts of North America, South America, Europe, Asia, and Australia, and together they make up the temperate forest biome. We recognize these regions by their broadleaf, deciduous trees and distinct seasons with warm summers and cold winters. **Deciduous** trees lose their leaves in autumn. Without their leaves to absorb sunlight they become **dormant**, or inactive, through the cooler months. Some animals also become dormant during winter as they **hibernate** in a protected area when there is not as much food available for them. Similar to a deep sleep, hibernation helps animals conserve energy to survive during winter. Other animals migrate to warmer areas with more resources when it's cold, and some animals stay active in the temperate forest through all the seasons.

Words from the Wild

Herbivore: an organism that eats plants

Carnivore: an organism that eats animals

Omnivore: an organism that eats both plants and animals

Decomposer: an organism that gets energy by breaking down dead and decaying plants and animals

Reproduce: the process by which a species makes more of its kind

Photosynthesis: the process plants (and some other organisms) use to produce their own food using sunlight, carbon dioxide, and water

Chlorophyll: a chemical in plants that helps them absorb the Sun's energy and gives them their green color

001 CAN YOU IDENTIFY THE LEVELS OF THE FOREST?

Forests have several layers, starting with the tallest trees in the **canopy**. The **understory**, made up of shorter trees and young trees, is just below the canopy. Woody-stemmed plants grow in the **shrub layer**, and softer-stemmed plants make up the **herb layer** below that. The **forest floor** is the layer that's covered in mosses, fallen leaves, lichens, rocks, and logs.

Can you label each layer of the forest ecosystem?

canopy | herb layer | shrub layer | the forest floor | understory

002 CAN YOU FIND LIFE IN A ROTTING LOG?

A rotting log on the forest floor is in itself a mini ecosystem. Most of the life you'll find on a rotting log is working to decompose it. Color and label the rotting log with the decomposers and any other living things you see.

Here's what you should look for:

ants	**ferns**	**grass**	**snail**
beetle	**fungi**	**moss and lichen**	

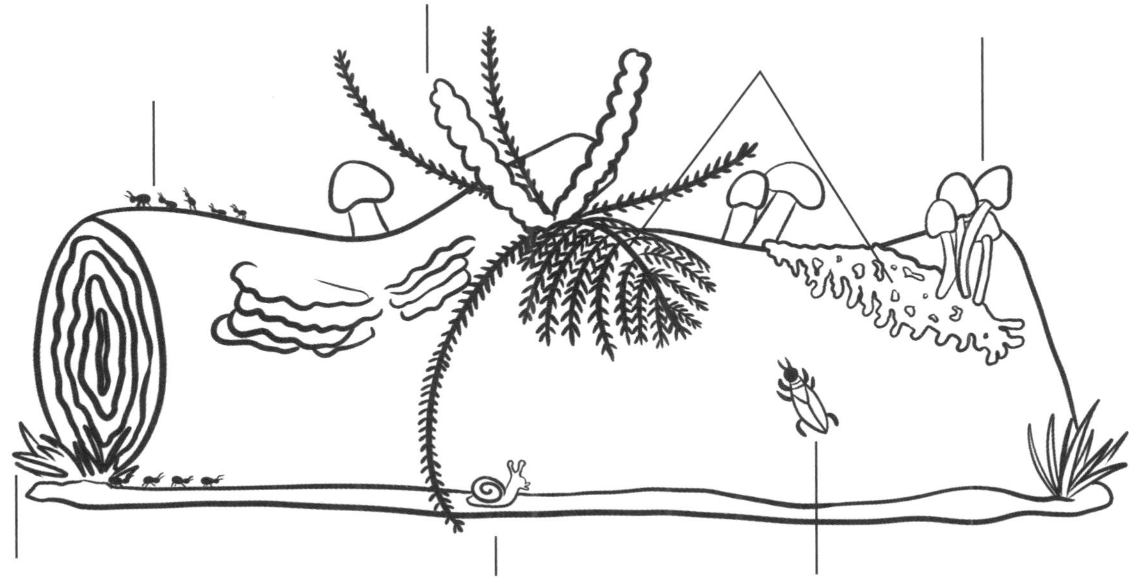

Did You Know? Ecosystems are communities of living and nonliving things working together. The living things, or biotic factors, in the temperate forest may include plants, animals, fungi, bacteria, and other microscopic organisms. Nonliving, or abiotic, parts of an ecosystem also play an important role in the healthy functioning of a temperate forest. Water, sunlight, soil, rocks, and air provide habitat, nutrients, and other vital components the living things need to survive.

Let's Explore! On your next nature walk, name all the living and nonliving things you can see, hear, touch, and smell around you.

003 CAN YOU COLOR THE SEASONS?

Deciduous trees drop their leaves to help them survive the colder months. Without leaves, trees are able to conserve their energy through the harsh winters of the temperate forest. Can you color the different sections of the tree below as it changes throughout the year?

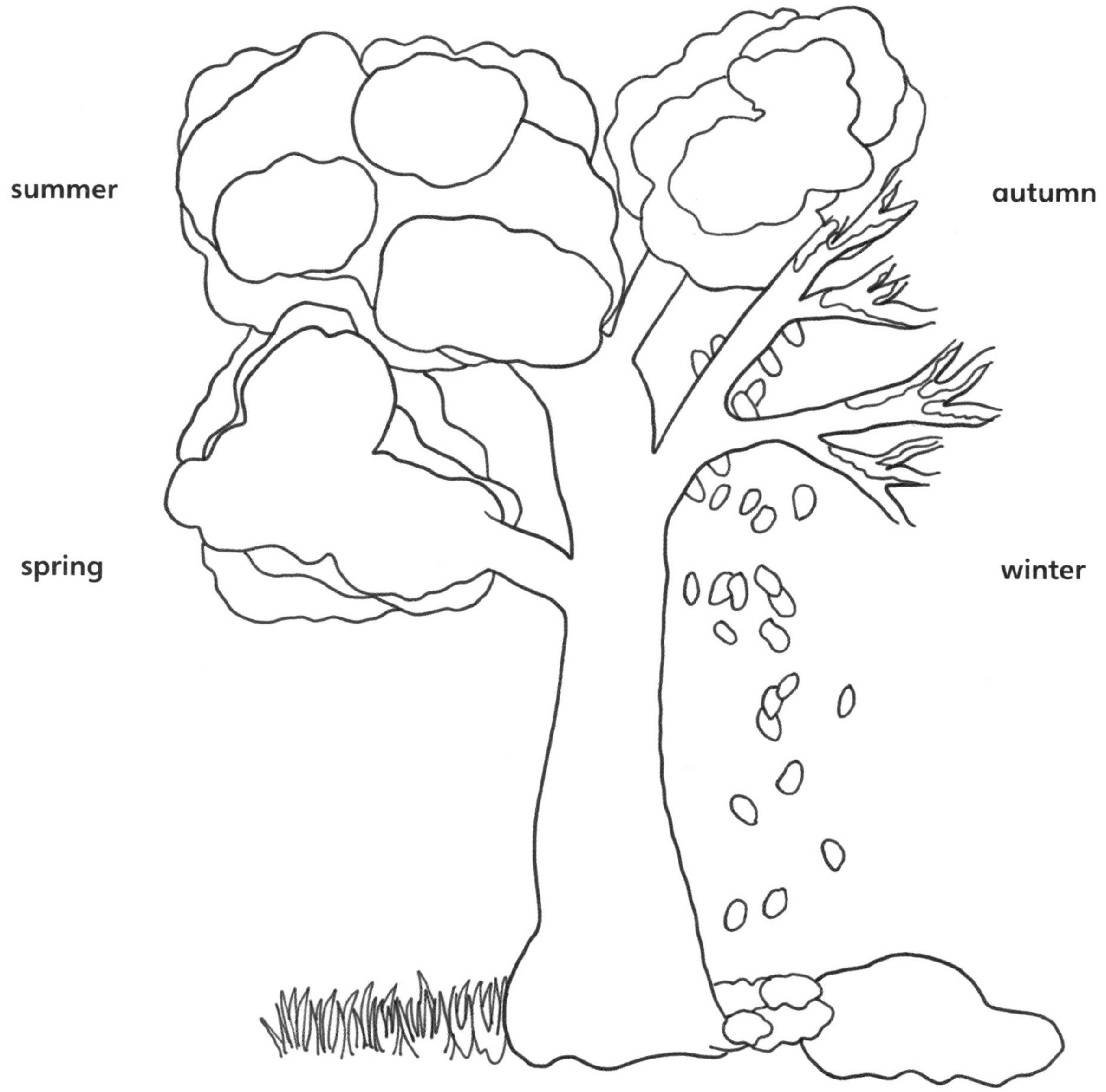

Did You Know? Chlorophyll is what gives leaves their green color. When leaves stop producing chlorophyll in autumn, the other hues come shining through.

004 WHAT IS TRANSPIRATION?

Water cycles through plants through a process called transpiration. The plant absorbs water from the ground, and the water is transported up through the plant. When it reaches the leaves, some water is lost through openings called stomata as water vapor escapes into the atmosphere.

Let's Explore! You might not be able to see the stomata on a leaf, but you can see the gas the stomata release. Place a fresh leaf from a plant into a glass of water. Watch for bubbles to form on the leaf as it releases oxygen through its stomata. Draw and describe your observations in the space below.

005 WHAT DO YOU KNOW ABOUT DECIDUOUS TREES?

Can you match deciduous tree-themed vocabulary with the correct definition?

broadleaf	a tree or plant with wide flat leaves
chlorophyll	falling off or shedding seasonally
deciduous	process used by plants to convert sunlight into energy
dormant	responsible for the green color of many plants
photosynthesis	the suspension or slowing down of physical functions for a period of time

Let's Explore! Visit a tree in your yard or favorite nature space. Identify the features of the tree. Return to your tree throughout the year to see how it changes with the seasons.

006 TREE BARK RUBBINGS

Tree bark comes in a variety of colors and may be completely smooth or have ridges or cracks. Bark can also look shaggy due to peeling strips, or it may appear scaley with hard plates. Bark can help us identify tree species!

Bark Type

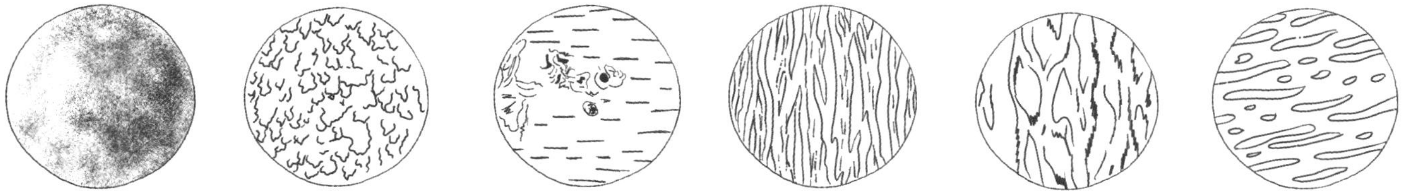

Smooth | **Scales** | **Peeling** | **Ridges** | **Plates** | **Lenticels**

Let's Explore! Place this page directly on the bark of different trees and rub a crayon on the paper to produce images of the bark underneath. Try to identify the tree species based on the bark type.

007 WHAT IS THE DIFFERENCE BETWEEN DECIDUOUS AND EVERGREEN TREES?

Most trees fall into one of two categories: deciduous or evergreen. Evergreen trees keep their leaves year-round. This is in contrast to deciduous trees, which drop their leaves each winter. Many evergreen trees have needle-shaped leaves and produce cones while many deciduous trees have broad leaves and produce flowers.

Let's Explore! Go on a nature walk to get an up-close look at both deciduous and evergreen trees. Then, complete the Venn diagram to compare and contrast them. One circle should contain the characteristics of deciduous trees while the other highlights the characteristics of evergreen trees. The overlapping space in the middle should include features shared by both.

008 HOW DO TREES GROW?

Deciduous trees are angiosperms, which means their seeds are contained in a "vessel" within a flower. When their seeds land in a suitable spot, they send roots into the ground to hold them in place. Then, a shoot forms and eventually grows into a seedling above the ground. It usually takes many years for the seedling to become a mature tree.

Even the mightiest of oaks begins its life as a tiny seed. Label the diagram below by writing each number next to each stage of the life cycle of an oak tree.

1.	2.	3.	4.	5.
acorn	seedling	sapling	young tree	mature oak tree

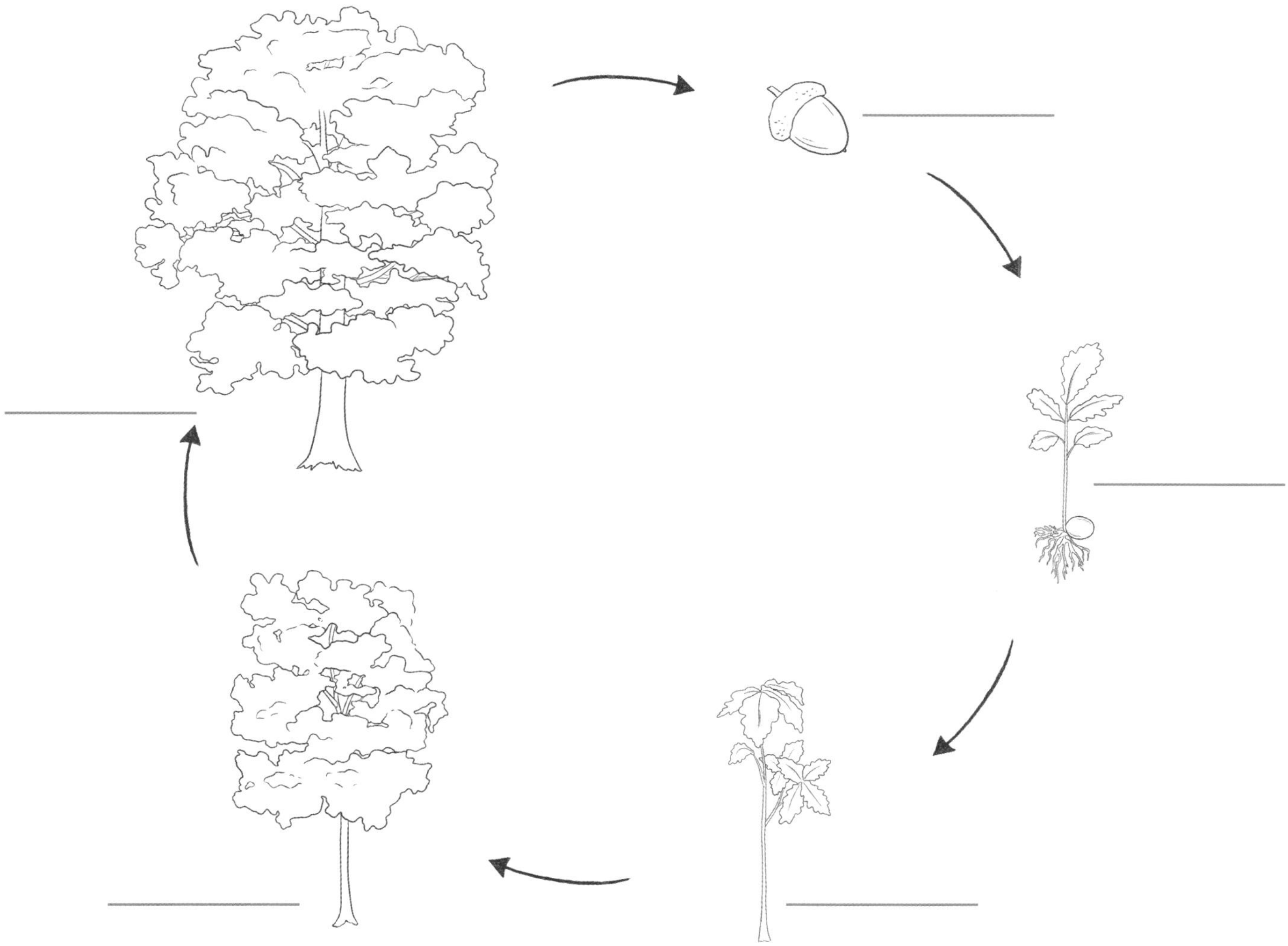

Let's Explore! Next time you're outdoors, try to identify an oak tree and look for acorns on its branches or on the ground underneath.

009 LET'S EXPLORE PHOTOSYNTHESIS!

Through photosynthesis, plants produce the food they need to survive. Plants take in carbon dioxide and water from their surroundings. Sunlight provides the energy plants need to make sugars from the carbon dioxide and water they have taken in. During photosynthesis, plants also create oxygen that is released into the atmosphere through tiny openings in their leaves.

Let's Explore! Can you write a recipe for photosynthesis? Be sure to include a list of "ingredients" needed for photosynthesis to take place along with how the ingredients combine to make food for the plant.

INGREDIENTS:

Sunlight
Water
Oxygen
Carbon Dioxide
Glucose (Sugars)

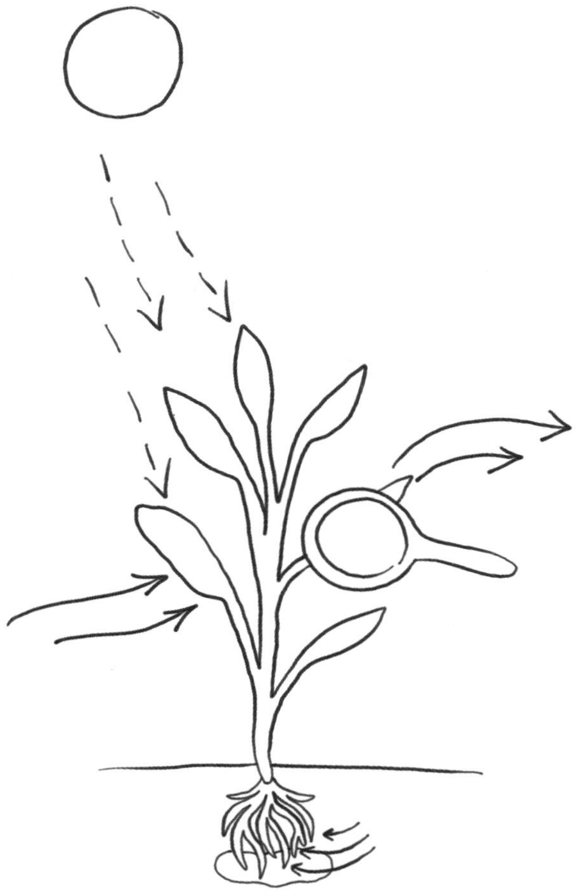

Recipe for Photosynthesis

010 IS THERE A FUNGUS AMONG US?

In the temperate forest, fungi serve as decomposers and provide food for both wildlife and people. Mushrooms and other fungi can be found dotting the ground, clinging to tree trunks and branches, and growing on fallen logs. Color the mushroom while you review its different structures.

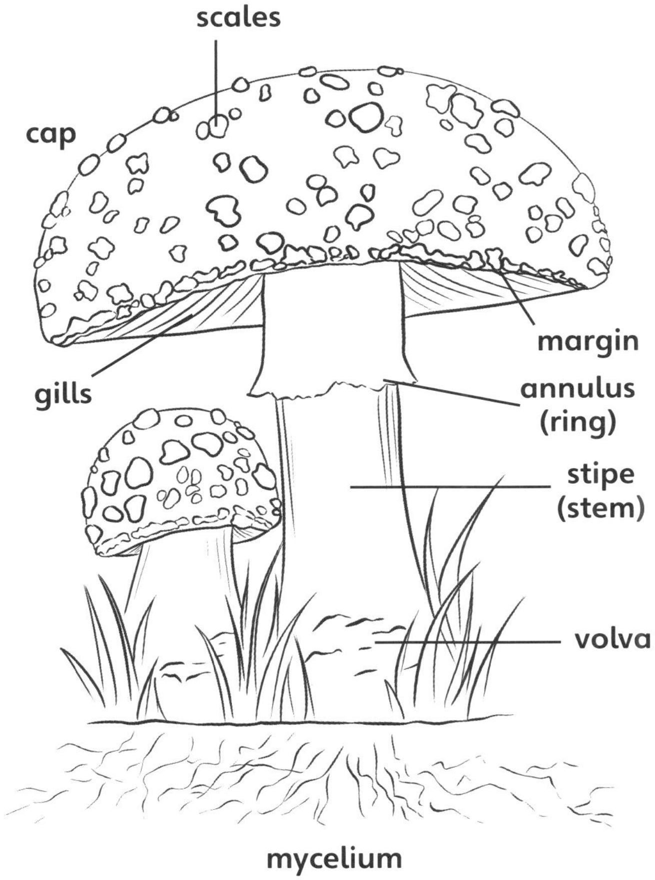

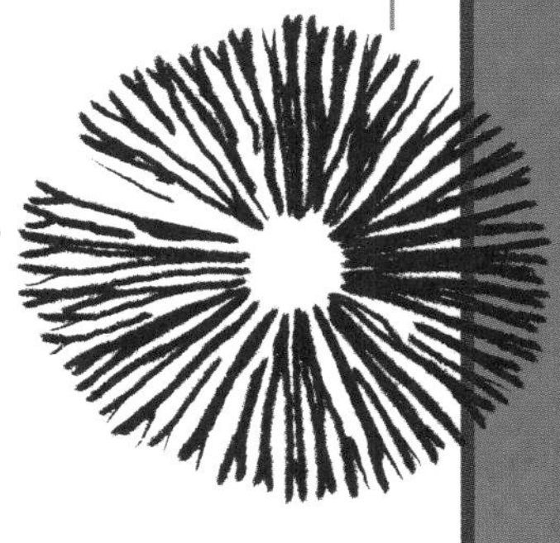

Let's Explore! Mushrooms reproduce by dispersing tiny spores from their gills. You can create a mushroom spore print by placing a mushroom cap gill-side down in the space provided. Cover and leave it undisturbed overnight. The next day, you should have a beautiful spore print on this page!

**If you have selected a mushroom with white or light-colored spores, you'll need to use dark paper to see your spores. In that case, you can tape the paper to the space above.*

011 DO YOU WANT TO BE A NATURE DETECTIVE?

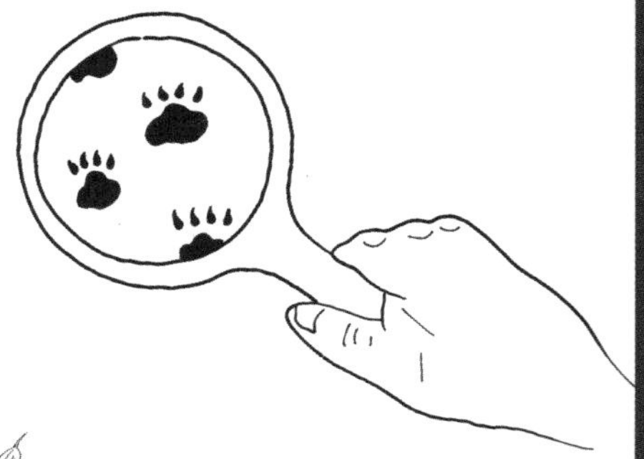

Often we don’t see the creatures that live in the temperate forest because they are great at hide and seek. But sometimes we can spot their tracks on the ground so we know what animals have visited that area.

Take a look at the illustrations of different forest fauna and try to match them to the correct track.

012 WINTER HOMES: TRUE OR FALSE

Many animals don't stick around for the winter season, migrating to warmer weather and plentiful food resources. Of those who remain, many hunker down in dens or sheltered areas.

Which statements are true about winter in the temperate forest?

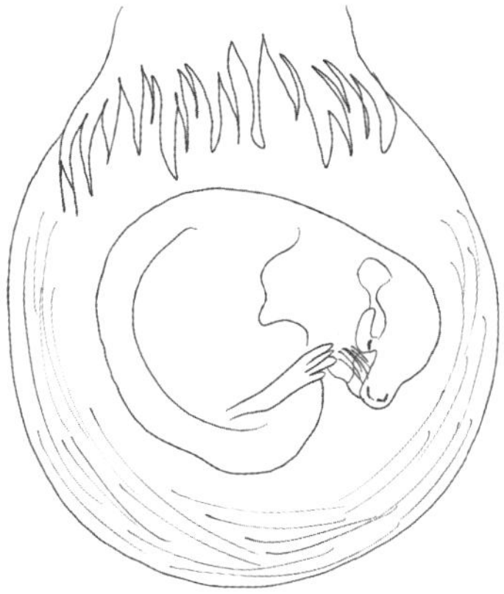

T or F Animals that live in the temperate forest must be adapted to the changing seasons, including hot temperatures in the summer months and cold temperatures in the winter months.

T or F All temperate forest animals hibernate through the winter.

T or F Many animals that live in the temperate forest in the summer migrate to warmer regions to avoid the winter.

T or F Winter in the temperate forest can include cold and snow.

T or F Hibernating animals may go to a protected area in winter when there is not as much food available for them.

T or F Plants and animals use a lot of energy during dormancy.

Let's Explore! Build your own winter shelter! You can go outside to find a spot that would make a suitable shelter or build one in the comfort of your own home. As you build, consider what an animal might need to keep warm and dry during the winter months.

013 WHAT MAKES UP A TEMPERATE FOREST FOOD CHAIN?

For the temperate forest to be a balanced ecosystem, both predators and prey must exist. Predators are animals that hunt and eat other animals, and prey are the animals that are hunted. Through their actions as hunters, predators help the entire ecosystem survive by keeping herbivorous animal populations in check.

Create your own forest food chain in the space provided. Draw pictures, then describe each link in the chain.

Let's Explore! Go on a nature walk and try to find a forest food chain in action. Maybe you'll see a squirrel with a nut or a bird catching a worm. Look for predators and prey as well as herbivores feeding on plants.

014 HOW TO DRAW A BEAR

1. Start by sketching simple circles and ovals to help you find the general shape and position of your bear.

2. Next, connect those shapes by adding the outline for your bear.

3. Add some details to your bear such as ears, nose, and eyes. Now is a good time to erase your sketched guidelines.

4. Continue to add details to your bear's face. Be sure to include features such as fur and claws.

5. Once you're happy with your drawing, define your lines by pressing firmly with your pencil or with an ink pen.

YOUR TURN!

Did You Know? Bears are usually omnivorous, meaning they eat both plants and animals, although some species eat more vegetation than others.

015 CAN YOU IDENTIFY THESE BIRD NESTS?

Flying through the forest, hopping around on the forest floor, perching, nesting, hunting, and foraging are all things birds do in the temperate forest biome. The temperate forest supports such diversity because of the different resources available.

Can you identify these different types of bird nests by matching the picture to the correct nest description?

scrape

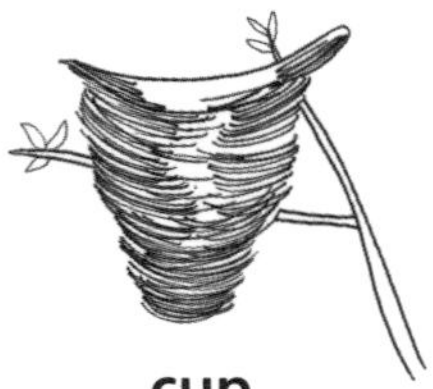

cup

mound

pendant

cavity

a pile of materials built in a depression on the ground

a shallow hole in the ground lined with sticks and other materials

an elongated pouch suspended from a tree branch

built in natural hollows such as trees cavities

cup-shaped with a deep rounded hollow in the center

Let's Explore! Build a bird nest of your own using materials you find in nature. Just like birds, you can use mud, twigs, grasses, leaves, moss, and string.

016 ARE YOU FAMILIAR WITH SONGBIRD ANATOMY?

Songbirds like tits, wrens, jays, finches, sparrows, warblers, and others in the order Passeriformes are common forest residents.

Color and label the songbird (great tit) using the words below.

beak: primarily used for gathering and eating food

claws: hard, curved nails on the feet

crown: top of the head

lore: between the eye and the beak

nape: the back of the neck

tail: at the rear and covered with feathers

tarsus: between toes and ankle

wing: forelimbs, key to flight

wing bar: stripe on upper wing

Let's Explore! Familiarize yourself with the songs of the birds in your region. Go on a nature walk to locate and identify bird species by their songs. Be sure to record the birds you identify in your nature journal!

017 HOW DO AMPHIBIANS REPRODUCE?

Many amphibians begin their lives looking quite differently than they do as adults. A major transformation called metamorphosis takes place as they grow.

Read the facts about the salamander life cycle. Color and label each by writing the correct number next to the stages.

1. eggs **2. larvae** **3. larvae with limbs** **4. adult salamander**

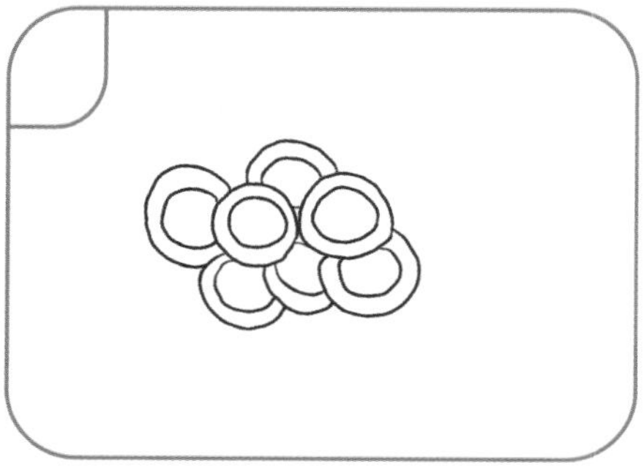

Jellylike eggs are laid in a clump on stones in freshwater.

Once hatched, larvae use their tails to wiggle through the water, looking for food.

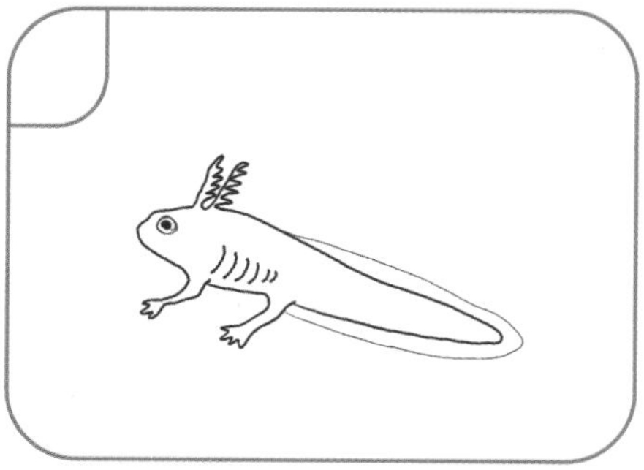

Larvae develop legs and lungs in preparation for living on land.

The adult transitions into a terrestrial life living under rotting logs and rocks.

Let's Explore! During the spring months, when the weather begins to warm up and rains bring moisture to the forest, look for amphibian eggs and tadpoles on your nature walks. Near pond edges and in wetlands are clever places to look for the jellylike masses of eggs or tiny larvae.

018 DO YOU HAVE A FAVORITE TEMPERATE FOREST REPTILE OR AMPHIBIAN?

With the scattered leaves, rocks, plants, and logs on the forest floor, reptiles and amphibians can seek shelter easily and find areas to make nests or overwinter. Write a report about a reptile or amphibian you have seen on your nature walks or you might find in the temperate forest.

NAME OF SPECIES:

DRAW THE SPECIES:

DESCRIBE ITS APPEARANCE:

WHAT DOES IT EAT?

WHAT IS ITS HABITAT LIKE?

DESCRIBE ITS LIFE CYCLE:

019 WHERE DO SPIDERS WEAVE THEIR TANGLED WEBS?

Many species of spider are found in the temperate forest. While we often associate spiders with webs, not all spiders make them. Those who do might construct them near the ground to catch crawling creatures, and others place their webs up high to catch flying bugs.

While outdoors, look for two sturdy sticks on the ground that have at least one fork in each so you can create your web. Use twine or string to wrap around the branching sections of your sticks in a weblike pattern.

1

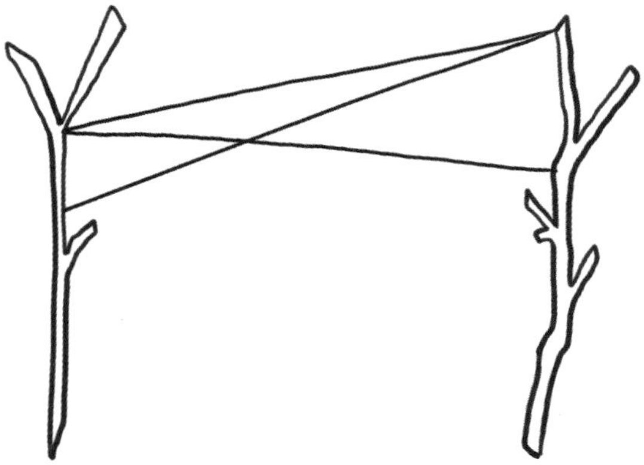

2

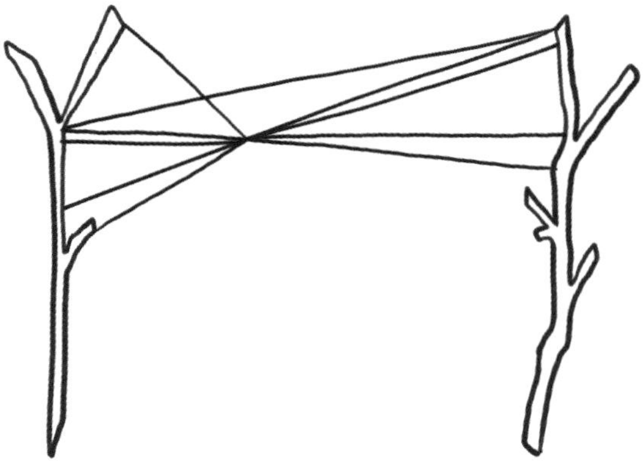

3

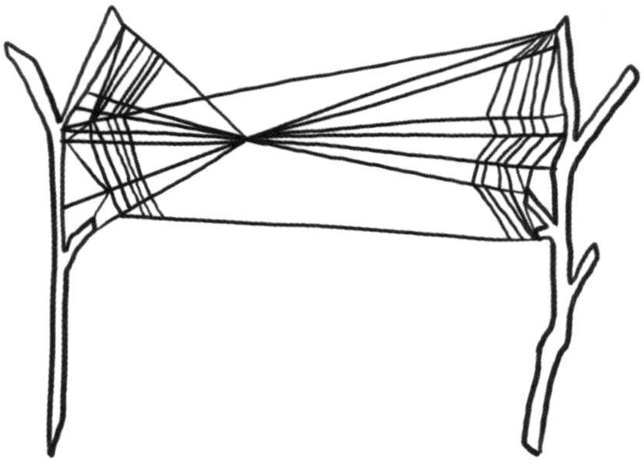

Let's Explore! See if you can find any spider webs in your yard or while exploring your favorite nature space.

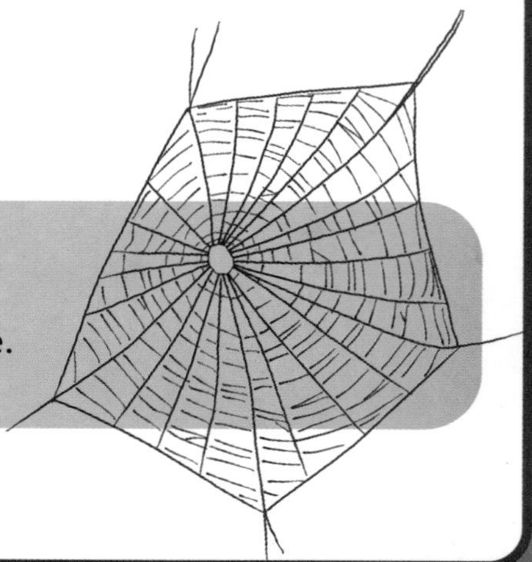

020 ARE YOU READY TO TAKE A WALK ON THE WILD SIDE?

Go outdoors to your favorite nature path and look for evidence that animals have been sharing the trail with you. We learned about animal tracks earlier, but there are plenty of other signs to look for in addition to footprints. Scat (animal poop), fur, holes in tree bark and on the ground, shed antlers or skin, bedding areas, and other wildlife markings provide clues to what animals are in an area. Write about and illustrate what you see!

021 TEMPERATE FOREST QUIZ

Test your knowledge by answering these questions using the word bank below.

1. What is the highest level in a forest? ____________
2. These organisms help break down dead organic material. ____________
3. What are the non-living parts of an ecosystem called? ____________
4. What do you call the four cyclical periods a year in a temperate forest? ____________
5. What is the chemical that gives leaves their green color? ____________
6. What is the process by which water cycles through plants? ____________
7. What type of tree drops its leaves during the autumn season? ____________
8. What is the protective outer layer of a tree trunk called? ____________
9. What is the first stage of life of oak trees? ____________
10. This is the process by which plants make their own food using sunlight. ____________
11. Mushrooms belong to this group of living things. ____________
12. Forest creatures may leave these behind as they walk the forest floor. ____________
13. What is it called when animals go dormant in winter? ____________
14. What term refers to animals that are hunted by predators? ____________
15. Bears usually eat both plants and animals, making them what kind of animal? ____________
16. Many birds use mud, twigs, grasses, leaves, moss, and string to construct these. ____________
17. What is the larval stage of an amphibian? ____________
18. What do some spiders build to catch flying bugs? ____________
19. These trees keep their leaves year-round. ____________
20. What is the term for wild animal poop? ____________

abiotic	**deciduous**	**nests**	**seasons**
acorn	**decomposers**	**omnivore**	**tadpole**
bark	**evergreen**	**photosynthesis**	**tracks**
canopy	**fungi**	**prey**	**transpiration**
chlorophyll	**hibernate**	**scat**	**web**

2

DESERTS

Discover!

DISCOVER!

With impressive landforms and vast expanses, the desert biome can be found on all continents around the world. Hot, sandy deserts like the Sahara have warm daytime temperatures most of the year, while semi-arid deserts and coastal deserts may be more mild. Cold deserts, like Antarctica, are chilly for most of the year. Regardless of their location, all deserts are **arid**, meaning they are dry and have little precipitation to offer the plants and animals that live there. Because of the extreme conditions in deserts, they are home to some species that are not found in any other place on Earth.

Invertebrates, animals without backbones such as insects and arachnids, are found in desert ecosystems. Most classes of **vertebrates** are common to deserts as well. These are animals with backbones and may include feathery **birds** such as falcons and roadrunners, scaly **reptiles** like lizards and tortoises, and furry **mammals** such as hyenas and mountain lions. Even **amphibians**, such as frogs and toads covered in moist skin, can be found burrowing in deserts.

Certain species of animals and plants are able to live in the desert because of their adaptations for aridity. **Adaptations** can be behaviors or physical features that allow living things to survive in their ecosystem. Some examples of desert adaptations are succulent plants that store water in their stems or plants that extend their roots deep into the ground to reach water stores. Animals may be **nocturnal**, coming out at night to avoid the Sun during the day, or they may have physical adaptations like large ears to radiate heat and keep them cool.

Words from the Wild

Weathering: breaking down of rock from exposure to the environment

Erosion: movement of sediment by wind and water

Landform: a surface feature of Earth such as dunes or mountains

Precipitation: water that falls to Earth in the form of rain, sleet, snow, and hail

Xerocoles: animals with adaptations to survive in the desert

Pollination: process of transferring pollen from the male part of a plant to the female part

Predator: animals that hunt other animals called prey

Prey: animals that are hunted by predators

022 HOW DOES DAY DIFFER FROM NIGHT IN THE DESERT?

In hot deserts, the difference between the hot days and cool nights can be extreme. Because deserts lack moisture in the air, the ground quickly heats up with the sunlight and then cools just as quickly without it. This means that many animals and plants are more active at night to avoid the heat of the day.

Color the illustration below, coloring one half as day and the other as night. Add a few plant and animal species of your own!

Let's Explore! Take a thermometer with you outside on a sunny day and set it down in direct sunlight. When the temperature on the thermometer is stable, read and record it in your nature journal. At night, when the Sun goes down, take your thermometer back outside to the same location. Record the temperature. Were they the same?

023 WHAT DO ALL DESERTS HAVE IN COMMON?

Different kinds of deserts exist throughout the world. The four major types of deserts include hot and dry deserts, semiarid deserts, coastal deserts, and cold deserts. Each type is unique, but all deserts share one thing in common: They receive little precipitation, making them extremely arid ecosystems.

Let's Explore! Take some time to learn about these desert ecosystems. Compare and contrast each type. What do they have in common? What makes them different?

Hot and Dry Deserts

Coastal Deserts

Similarities

Semiarid Deserts

Cold Deserts

024 HOW DO DESERTS FORM?

Deserts are formed through weathering processes. While you may think of rocks as indestructible, they actually break down over time. Weathering is usually slow in the desert simply because there's hardly any water to help it along.

In the chart below, match each type of weathering on the erosion diagram with the descriptions provided by writing the name of the process in the left column.

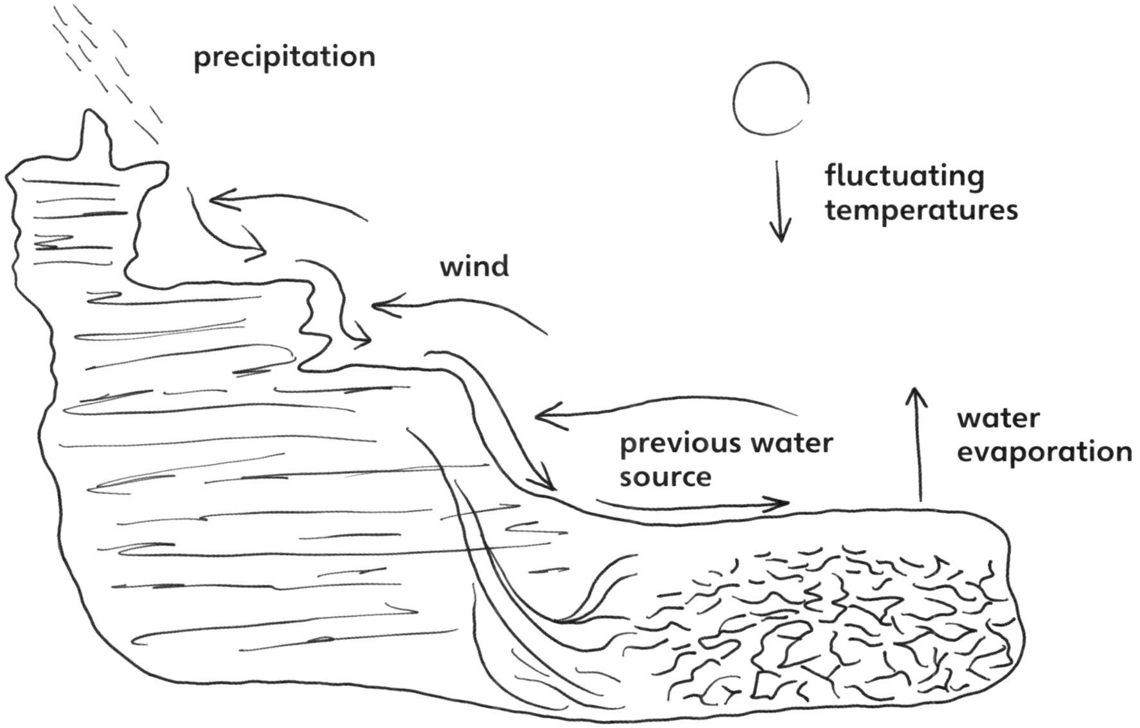

	Rapid heating of rocks by the Sun and then night time cooling leads to rocks breaking down as does freezing of water in rocky crevices.
	Drenching rains, although short-lived, can cause large amounts of debris and water to be carried down slopes, which also causes rocks to wear down.
	Dust and particles are blown through the air and across ground surfaces.
	Surface water can seep into cracks and crevices in rocks, exerting pressure on the rocks, causing them to weaken and eventually break apart.
	Salt and minerals left behind by water may gradually weaken and break down rock.

025 WHAT'S THAT LANDFORM?

The weathering process may be different in deserts compared to other habitats due to the overall lack of water, but it does help create some amazing landforms found in the desert biome. Study the illustrations and descriptions of the different desert landforms. Then, try making some of the landforms with blocks, clay, or any other materials you have at home.

alluvial fan: fan pattern of sediment formed when desert rains carry rocks, sand, or silt downhill

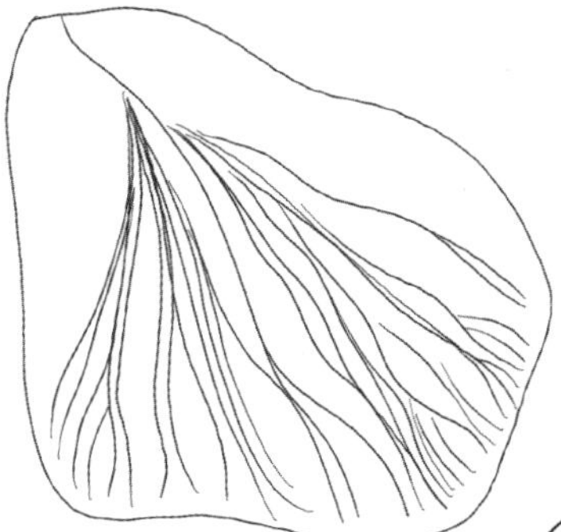

inselberg: hard rock mountains that form when softer rock around them wears away

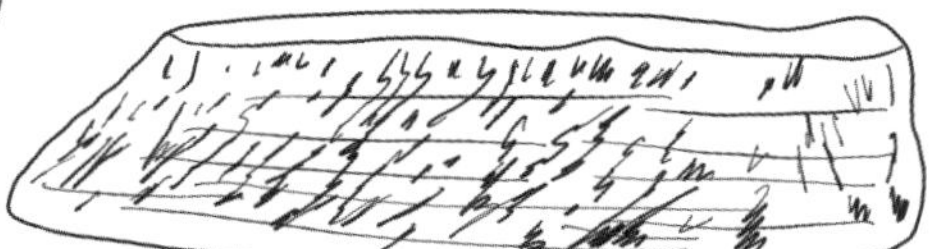

mesa: flat hill or mountain formed when wind and water wear away the rock on top

arch: opening in rock with a curved top; formed by weathering and wearing away of rock

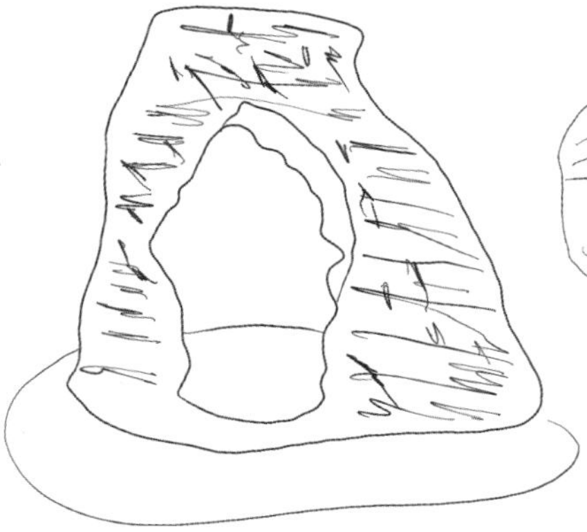

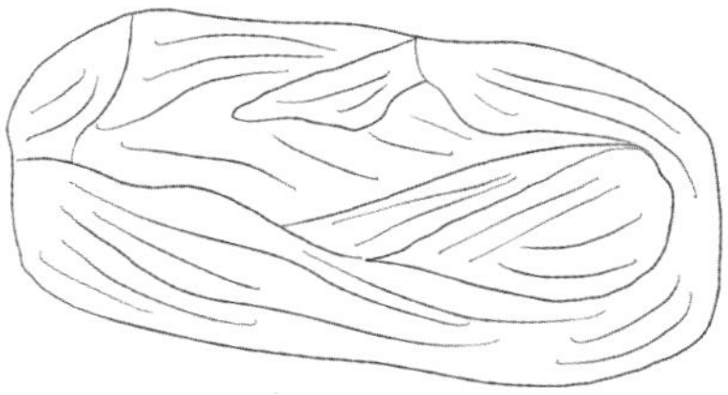

sand dune: hill of sand formed by the wind

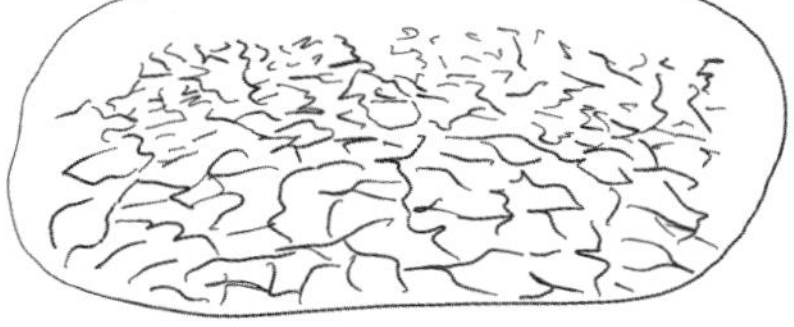

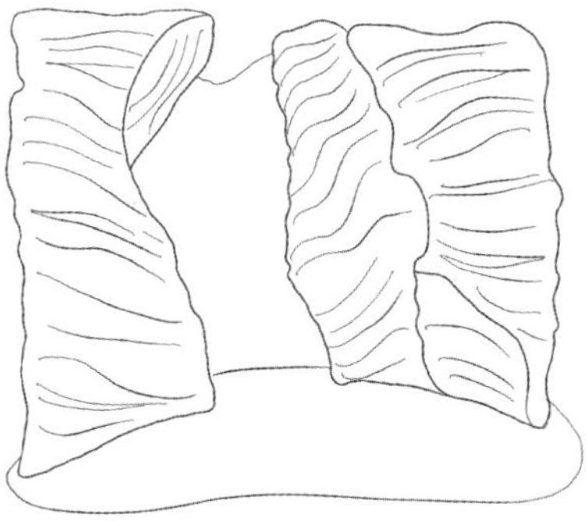

playa: dry basins that collect rain; cracked appearance during dry season

river canyon: deep channel formed in rock as water wears it away

026 CAN YOU DESCRIBE THE PARTS OF THE ROCK CYCLE?

The rock cycle is an ongoing process in which different types of rocks are weathered and eroded into sediment, moved around, and changed.

Igneous rocks are formed when **magma** cools below ground or on the Earth's surface. **Sedimentary rocks** form when layers of **sediment** are compacted and cemented together over time by pressure and heat. These forces also work to change the structure and minerals in rocks. We call the resulting rocks **metamorphic** because they have undergone change.

Let's Rock! Color and label the rock cycle diagram below using the word bank provided.

igneous rock **magma**

sediment **metamorphic rock**

sedimentary rock

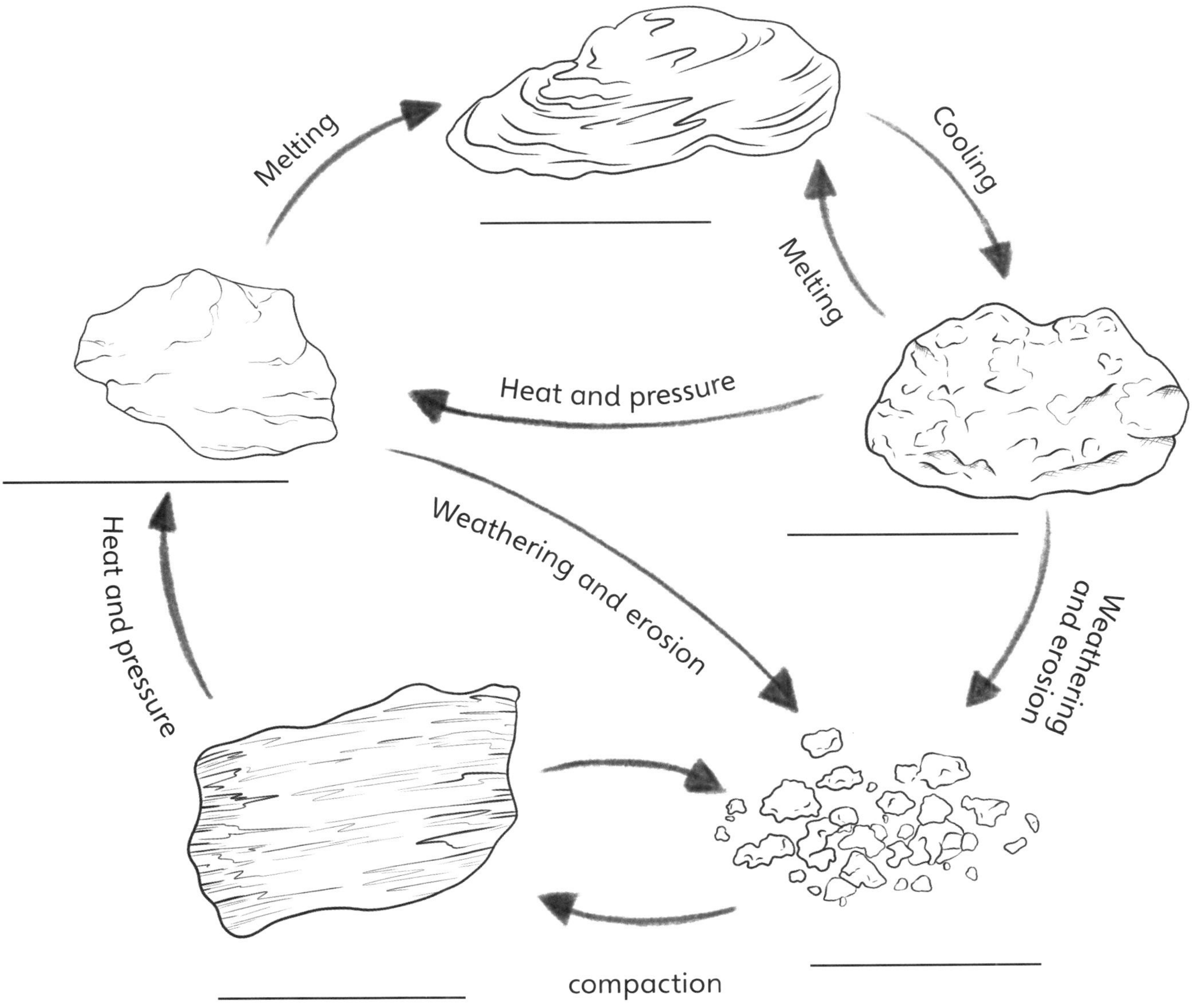

027 WHY ARE CACTI THE "DARLINGS" OF THE DESERT?

While not all deserts have cacti, they are an iconic image of hot, dry, sandy environments. Plus, they provide an important habitat for other species in the desert.

Color the cactus habitat below. Add in any additional wildlife you've learned about that would fit into the cactus habitat.

028 CAN YOU SOLVE THE POLLINATOR PUZZLE?

Plants are the base of the food chain in every biome, including deserts. Without pollinators, plants wouldn't grow to feed the animals of the desert. Plants wouldn't shade the ground, they wouldn't prevent soil erosion, and they wouldn't create oxygen for the Earth's inhabitants.

Use the drawings and hints to help you identify the different types of desert pollinators.

Hint: They are known to pollinate desert plants while migrating over long distances.

____

Hint: They have a strawlike mouth called a proboscis to help them drink nectar.

____

Hint: These and other bird species use their long beaks and tongues to drink nectar from flowers.

____

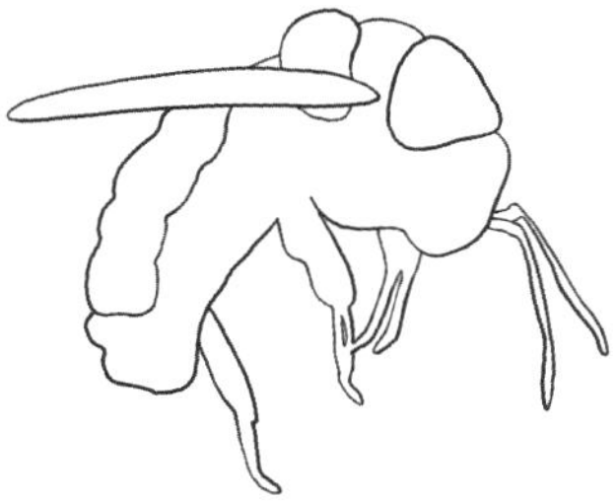

Hint: They enjoy eating both nectar and pollen from desert blooms.

____

Let's Explore! Go on a nature walk or explore your own backyard and look for pollinators. Flowers, gardens, and trees are great spots to find them!

029 HOW DOES A CACTUS GROW?

If the conditions are just right, a cactus will grow from a tiny seed that falls on the desert soil.

Read the facts about the cactus life cycle. Then, color each stage and label each box with the correct number.

1. seed **2. seedling** **3. juvenile** **4. mature flowering cactus**

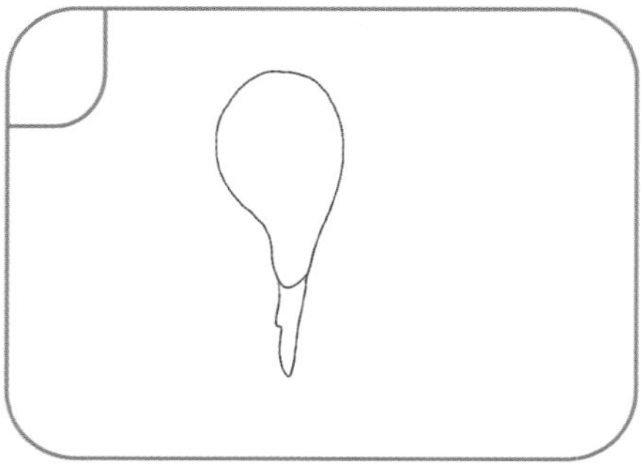

A seed germinates and sends out a taproot.

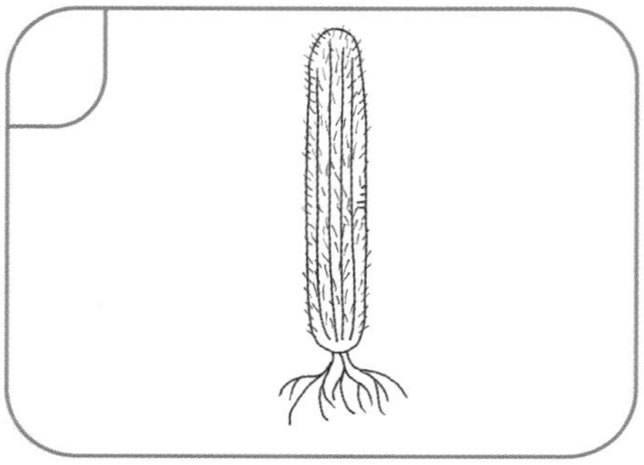

The plant grows and stores water, developing spines to protect itself.

New branches form and spring out from the main body of the plant.

Flowers bloom at the tips of the branches for pollinators to transform into fruit.

030 WHOOOOSE ADAPTATION IS IT?

Animals beat the desert heat by avoiding the Sun altogether. Hunting or foraging at night has its own set of factors to consider for these nocturnal animals.

Draw a line from the nocturnal animal to its correct adaptation.

large eyes

sense vibrations

echolocation

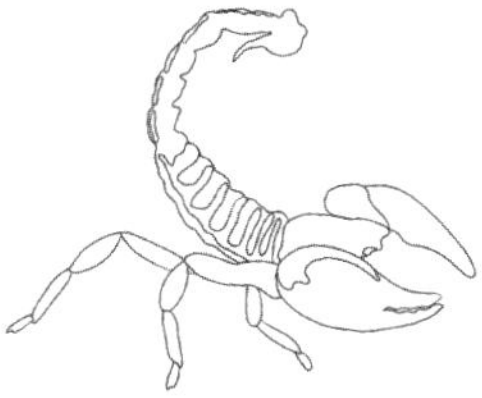

heat sensing pits

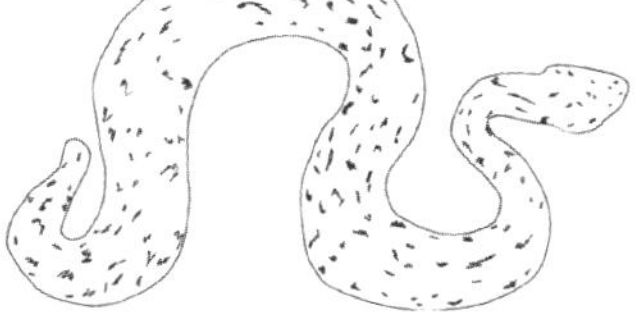

large ears

Let's Explore! What nocturnal animals live in your region? Take a night hike to discover nocturnal species. Here are some helpful tips for night hikes: 1. Make sure you go with a responsible adult. 2. Visit a familiar area. Even walking around your neighborhood can be fun! 3. Bring a flashlight. 4. Walk quietly and listen closely.

031 WHO LIVES IN THE DESERT?

Xerocoles are animals with adaptations to survive the arid desert conditions. While the desert heat and dryness can be relentless, there are many ways animals cope with life in the desert. Each species has a unique combination of adaptations to help it survive.

Below are some examples of xerocoles and their adaptation. Can you describe why their adaptation would be helpful in the desert?

OSTRICH'S LONG, POWERFUL LEGS

CAMEL'S HUMP THAT STORES FAT

JACKRABBIT'S LARGE EARS

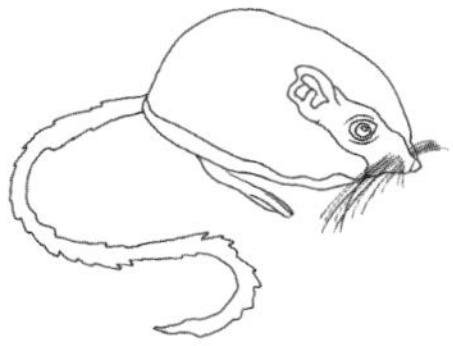

KANGAROO RAT'S LARGE BACK LEGS

WOLF'S SHORT FUR COAT

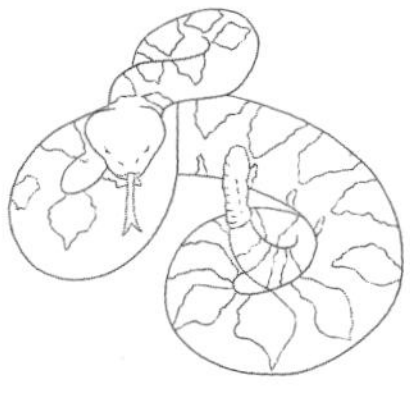

RATTLESNAKE'S CAMOUFLAGE PATTERN

032 CAN YOU CATEGORIZE THE DESERT ANIMALS?

Animals of all sorts are vital to the desert ecosystem. They play the role of carnivore, herbivore, or omnivore. Desert plants are important as well. They provide a source of food and sometimes water. Animals can get the water they need from desert succulents that store water in their stems, leaves, and fruit.

Look at the list of desert animals below and write the name of each animal in the appropriate category on the chart. Take this activity one step further and jot down the characteristics that animals in each category share.

bearded dragon	**frog**	**locust**	**scorpion**
big brown bat	**Gila monster**	**ostrich**	**sphinx moth**
cactus wren	**goanna**	**peregrine falcon**	**tarantula**
camel	**golden eagle**	**rattlesnake**	**toad**
centipede	**jackrabbit**	**roadrunner**	**tortoise**
fennec fox	**javelina**	**salamander**	

Amphibian	Bird	Invertebrate	Mammal	Reptile

033 WHO ARE THE POWERFUL PREDATORS IN THE DESERT?

Often, predators are larger species and are carnivores, though some are omnivores. In the desert food chain, prey are usually smaller herbivores such as mammals, reptiles, amphibians, birds, and insects. Sometimes, the hunter becomes the hunted, and predators fall prey to bigger, more powerful creatures.

Make your own desert food chain in the space provided. Choose a predator and prey, and don't forget the plants and sunlight that get everything started! Draw pictures and then describe each link in the chain.

034 CAN YOU SOLVE THIS RIDDLE ABOUT A DESERT PREDATOR?

It's a Mystery! This fairy-tale predator's diet includes small mammals, such as rodents and hares, as well as ungulates. It must have water to drink, so it lives near the edges of deserts where water is more accessible. Unlike some desert species, this crafty canine escapes the daytime heat by digging a den deep in the ground. And its beige coat blends right into the desert landscape.

Let's see if you can solve the riddle!

I don't hunt by
day or by night.
I venture out
when the Sun is
barely in sight.

People revere
me, but I give
them a scare.
I'm larger than
they think—small
animals beware.

I travel in a pack,
slinking with my
tail stretched
from my back.

Yes, I can
howl, but also
whine, whimper,
and bark. I
communicate
well using scent
as my mark.

My piercing eyes
are narrow and
my keen ears tall.
I use these to
spot prey while I
stealthily trawl.

DRAW A PICTURE OF THE MYSTERY DESERT PREDATOR:

035 WHAT ARE THE PARTS OF A BIRD WING?

Consider specific bird species and their wing shape and function. Songbirds may have small, rounded wings suited for taking flight quickly. Long, broad wings with long flight feathers, like those of eagles, are good for soaring. Narrow, pointed wings mean quick flight and maneuverability. Even with the variation in size and shape, most bird wings have the same types of feathers.

Color the bird wing and label the types of wing feathers with the corresponding number from the diagram.

_____ **PRIMARY FLIGHT FEATHERS:** largest flight feathers near the outer edge to help birds move through the air

_____ **SECONDARY FLIGHT FEATHERS:** extend from middle of wing to give the bird lift

_____ **COVERTS:** give shape to the wing and allow air to flow smoothly around the wing

Did You Know? Desert birds often get the water they need from the seeds, fruits, or animals they eat. In addition, they are able to conserve water because they eliminate very little liquid waste.

036 WANT TO WRITE ABOUT A RAPTOR?

Research birds of prey that live in your region. Then, go outside and search for them in the wild. Look for hawks perched on telephone poles or high in the trees. Watch for eagles soaring in the sky or swooping down to catch their prey. Listen for the hoot of an owl at night. Write a raptor report about a species in your region. Be sure to include any interesting facts you uncover in your research.

NAME OF SPECIES:

DRAW THE SPECIES:

DESCRIBE ITS APPEARANCE:

WHAT DOES IT EAT?

WHAT IS ITS HABITAT LIKE?

WHAT ARE ITS ADAPTATIONS?

037 WHY DO ANIMALS AESTIVATE?

You may be familiar with hibernation, or when animals become inactive during cold winter months. But have you heard of aestivation? It involves animals and inactivity, but the cold in hibernation is replaced with heat. Deserts can get so hot that it makes more sense for some animals to bury themselves in the ground and become dormant until temperatures cool and moisture returns. Body processes such as breathing and heart rate slow down, and very little energy is used by the animals.

Fill in the blanks using the words below to learn more about aestivation.

amphibians **dormant** **energy** **temperature** **underground**

1. Aestivation usually occurs when the ________________ is hot.

2. During aestivation, animals become ________________ because of the heat.

3. When they are dormant, animals use very little ________________.

4. Reptiles and ________________ in the desert may aestivate in order to survive.

5. Rock crevices and ________________ are two places where animals aestivate to escape the heat.

Did You Know? Amphibians, with their sensitive skin and their need to stay moist, have a challenging time in an arid desert. Some amphibian species even coat their bodies in special secretions or skin layers to keep moisture inside.

038 DO RATTLESNAKES LIVE IN THE DESERT?

Rattlesnakes are a highly venomous type of snake. They are distinguished by their different color patterns. Those that live in the desert usually have colors and designs on their scales that help them blend into the surrounding sand and rock. They are often nocturnal, using heat-sensing pits to detect warm-blooded prey and sensing vibrations in their surroundings, which helps them even in low-light conditions.

Can you match rattlesnake-themed vocabulary terms with the correct definition?

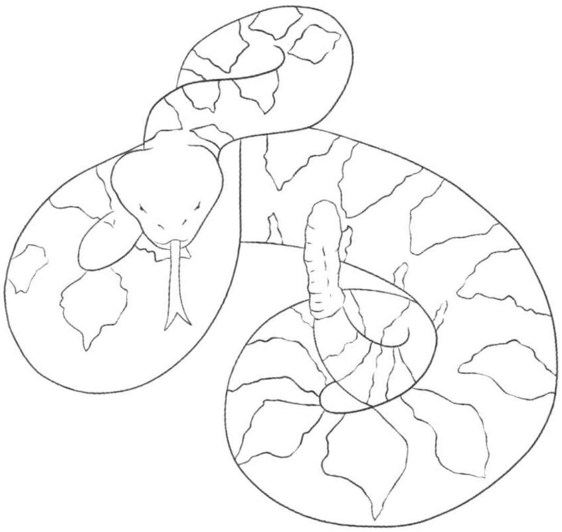

camouflage	a small, rigid protective plate that grows out of an animal's skin
cold-blooded	active at night and sleeps during the day
nocturnal	cold-blooded, air-breathing vertebrate with body covered in scales and/or scutes
reptile	defense tactic used to disguise appearance
scales	having a body temperature that varies with the environment
venom	highly toxic saliva containing toxins that immobilize prey

Did You Know? Rattlesnakes are able to feel vibrations from the ground with their bodies, and their tongues can smell prey as well.

039 CAN YOU MAKE YOUR WAY THROUGH THE MAZE?

Ant colonies often live in humid burrows they construct underground. The hill or mound forms the top part of the nest and houses the entrance. Inside, there are several chambers for eggs and larvae, food storage, the queen, and resting.

Help the ants find their way through the ant hill maze.

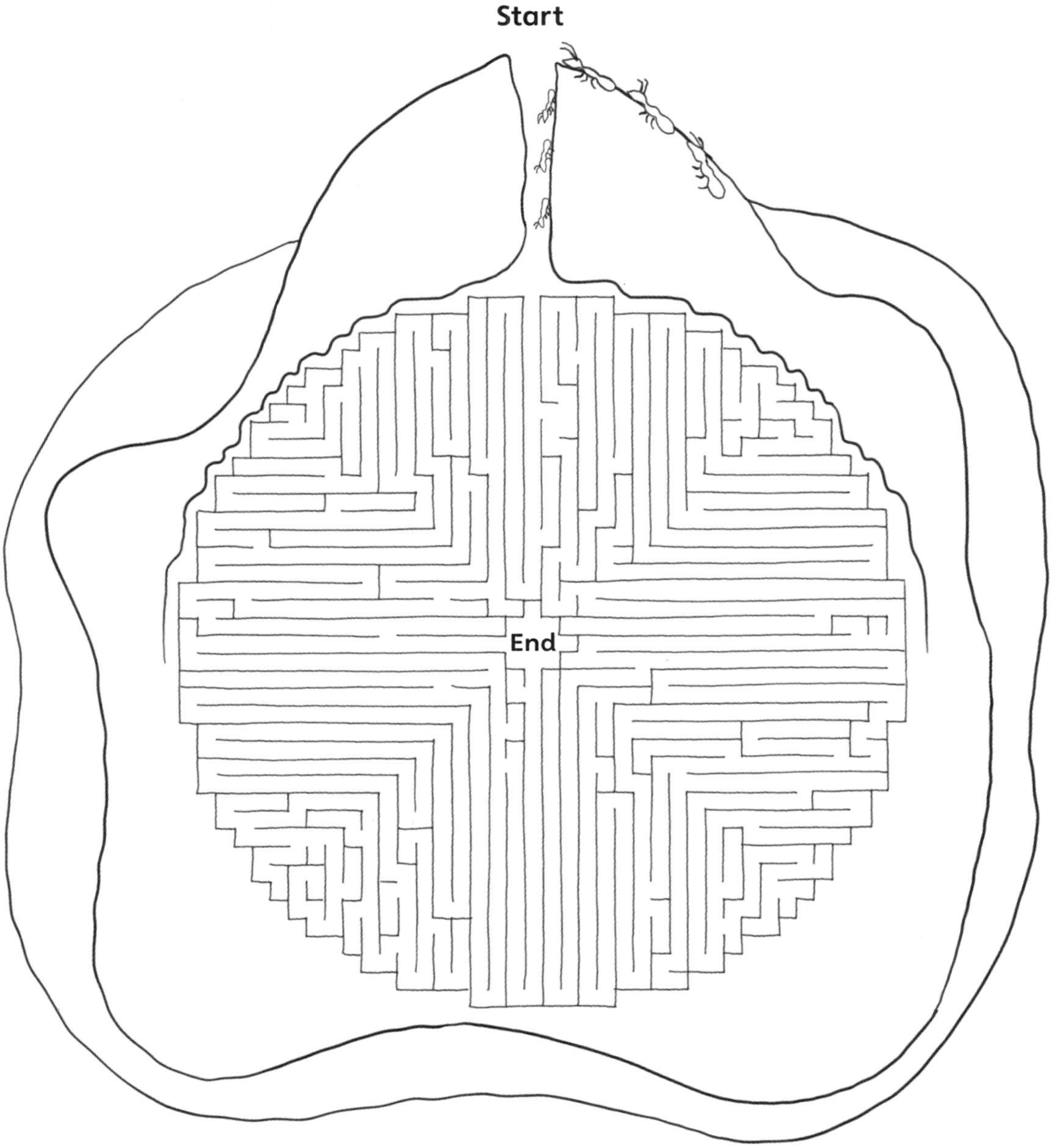

Let's Explore! On your next nature walk, look for an ant hill. Without disturbing the ants, observe them at work.

040 HAVE YOU EVER SEEN A MONARCH BUTTERFLY?

Monarch butterflies are easily recognized by their classic black, orange, and white wing design. They lay their eggs only on milkweed plants because that's what their larvae eat. Monarch populations in North America are famous for the migration many undertake each year. During their migration, monarchs go through desert regions, and flowers with nectar are essential for energy on their journey.

Color the monarch butterfly using those characteristic black, orange, and white colors. Label the key features of the butterfly such as wings, antennae, legs, head, thorax, and abdomen.

041 WHAT DO YOU SEE IN THE DESERT?

Visit a desert region, or read a book about deserts, and journal about this arid ecosystem. What did you observe? What plants and animals live there? How does this biome look and feel compared to others? Choose to write about the entire ecosystem, a single species, or something in between. Be sure to include an illustration along with the information you learned from your research and observations.

042 DESERT QUIZ

Test your knowledge by answering these questions using the word bank below.

1. This allows an animal to blend into its surroundings. ______________________
2. Which birds are commonly referred to as "birds of prey"? ______________________
3. What is the seasonal movement of animals from one region to another? ____________
4. What is the scientific term for the process of liquid transforming into vapor? ____________
5. What is the state some animals enter during periods of intense heat? ____________
6. What is the term used to describe an animal that hunts other animals? ____________
7. A canyon, arch, and inselberg are all types of what geological feature? ____________
8. What do you call animals that sleep during the day and are active at night? ____________
9. What is the specific term used to describe animals with adaptations to survive desert conditions? ______________________
10. These animals play a crucial role in aiding plants in seed formation and reproduction. ______________________
11. What is the process by which rocks break down over time by wind and water? ______________________
12. What spiny plant is adapted to life in the desert? ______________________
13. What type of rock is made from compacted sediment? ______________________
14. What type of rock is made from cooled magma? ______________________
15. Large eyes, heat-sensing pits, and echolocation are examples of what? ____________
16. What type of rock has undergone change? ______________________
17. What word describes the extremely dry climate of deserts? ______________________
18. What is the collective term for a group of ants? ______________________
19. What is the state of inactivity when normal physical functions are suspended or slowed down? ______________________
20. Animals may create these underground to escape the extreme weather of the desert. ______________________

adaptations	**cactus**	**erosion**	**metamorphic**	**predator**
aestivation	**camouflage**	**evaporation**	**migration**	**raptor**
arid	**colony**	**igneous**	**nocturnal**	**sedimentary**
burrows	**dormancy**	**landforms**	**pollinator**	**xerocole**

3

SEASHORE

Discover!

DISCOVER!

Maybe you have been to a seashore and experienced the pounding waves and shifting sands in all their brilliance. Maybe you have read about them in books and imagined visiting. Or maybe your knowledge of seashores is limited, and you look forward to learning more. Seashores are found around all the continents on Earth, anywhere land and ocean meet. With the variety of landscapes across the globe, it's no surprise that seashores have many different "faces" from jagged rocks or smooth sands to silty mud flats or sheer cliffs. The **biodiversity** in seashore ecosystems is high, meaning many types of plants and animals are represented. Water along the seashore is often shallow, but in the open ocean, it is much deeper. The open ocean is divided into zones by scientists based on how far the sunlight reaches, water temperature, and water depth. These characteristics influence the type of organisms able to live there.

On the shore, grasses and shrubs may anchor in the rocks or sand, while invertebrates like crabs scurry along the ground. Reptiles such as sea turtles, some marine mammals, and birds may use both land and sea while fish, octopuses, anemones, and more spend time in the coastal waters. Even microscopic plants and animals inhabit this area, and often algae forms the base of the seashore food chain. Small and large invertebrates as well as fish of different sizes become part of the food chain as well. **Apex predators** near the seashore include animals such as sharks and orcas. These are creatures that don't have natural predators in their ecosystem. At the top of the food chain, they help keep the seashore ecosystem in balance.

Words from the Wild

Coast: area of land next to the ocean

Shore: a general term for a strip of land near a body of water such as a lake or sea

Wave: energy moving through the water, often caused by wind

Tide: daily rise and fall of the ocean's water caused by the gravitational pull of the Moon and Sun

Fish: cold-blooded vertebrate animal that lives in water with fins for swimming, scales covering its body, and gills to breathe

Sand: formed from weathering of rocks and carried and deposited through the process of erosion

Ocean zones: a column of five zones in the ocean water, each with their own characteristics, from the sunlit epipelagic zone to the cold and dark hadalpelagic zone

043 WHAT ARE THE PARTS OF A BEACH?

Some areas of the beach are constantly submerged while others are underwater for only part of the day. The dry beach, farther inland, only receives sea spray and the occasional storm surge or spring tide. Next to this area, plant species such as grasses and shrubs may trap blowing sands to form dunes. In low-lying areas between dunes, trees may take root.

Using the word bank, label the illustration below with the different parts of a beach. Then, color the illustration.

backshore: usually dry area between dunes and the beach face

beach face: area of the shore exposed to the waves

high tide shoreline: where the tide advances during high tide

longshore trough: depression in sand between the beach and outer sandbar

low tide shoreline: the lowest part of the beach that is exposed during low tide

sand dunes: ridges of wind-blown sand

sandbar: submerged ridge of sand built by waves

vegetation: plants adapted to the shore, protects beach from erosion

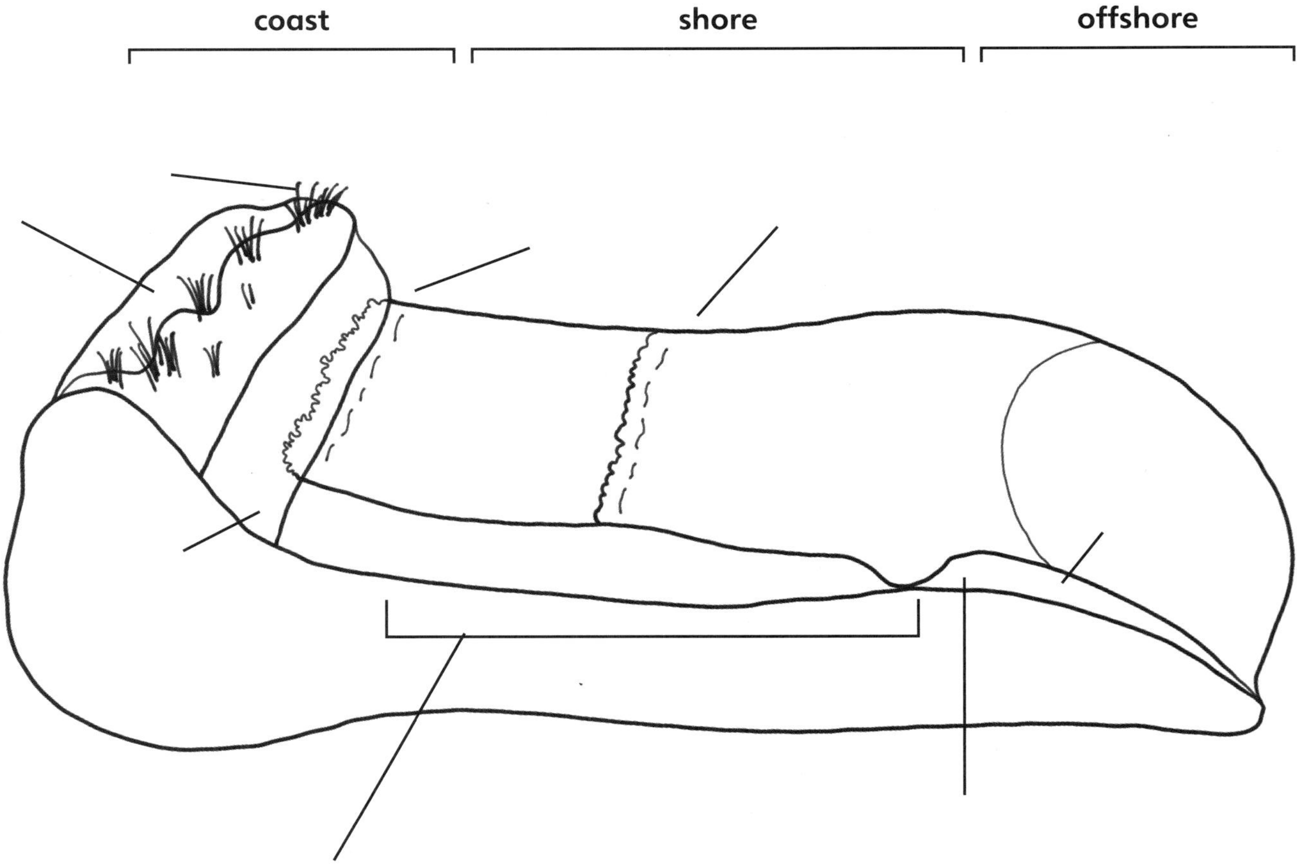

044 CAN YOU NAME THAT LANDFORM?

Landforms along the coast may be created by weathering and the erosion, or carrying away, of sediment. Alternatively, they may be formed when waves deposit sediment in an area.

Label each landform below using the words provided and briefly describe each based on your research.

Match the description of the seashore landforms and draw a line to the correct picture.

arches: rock formation created when caves in headlands wear away

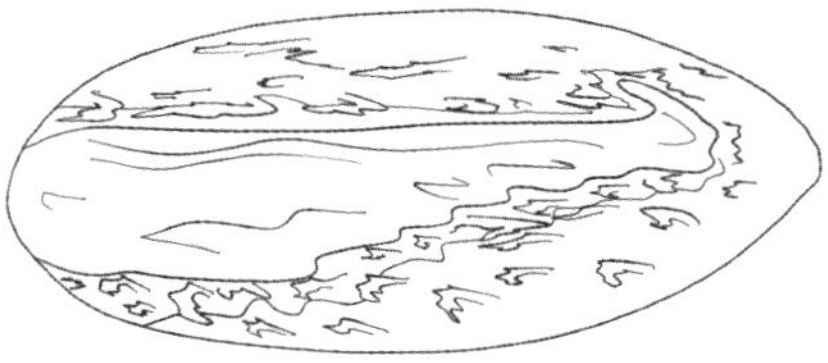

beaches: areas of sand, rocks, or mud deposited along the coast

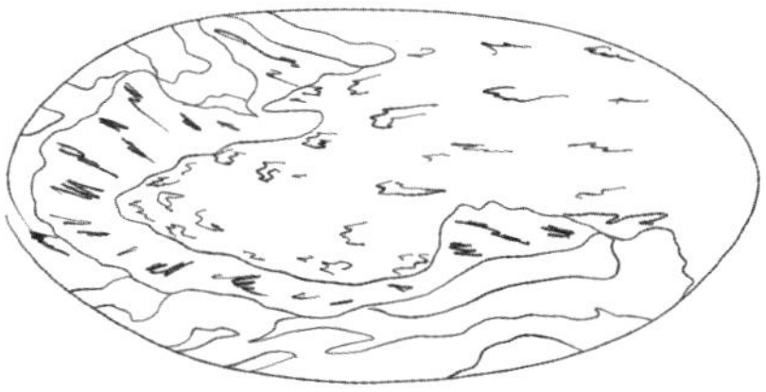

headlands: point of land created when areas of soft rock are worn away by the sea

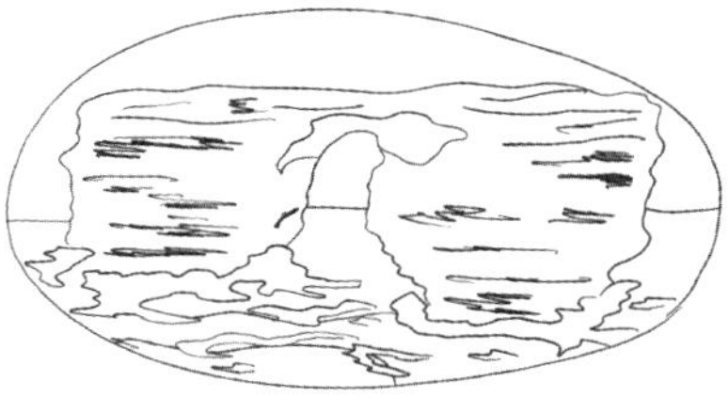

lagoon: protected, shallow areas of water fed by the ocean or rivers

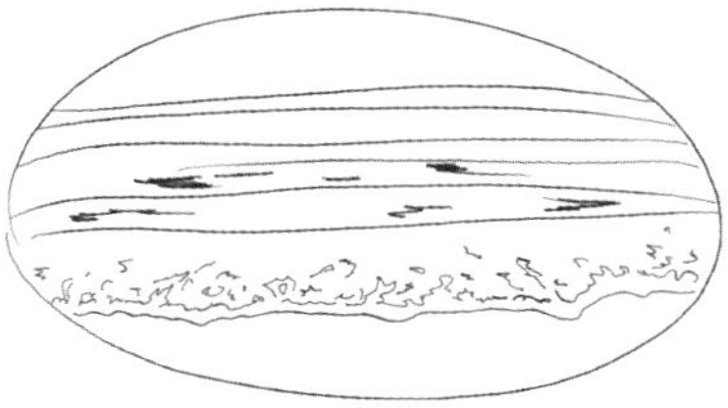

spit: collection of sediment created by longshore drift

tombolos: spits that bridge mainland to an island

045 WHAT DOES SAND LOOK LIKE WHEN IT'S MAGNIFIED?

Take a look at sand under a microscope. Use the sand you've collected from a beach trip or from your sandbox. Compare and contrast different types if you have more than one type available. What do you see? How do the sand types look different under the microscope versus with your naked eye? Report your findings below.

046 WHAT ROLE DO SAND DUNES PLAY?

Fill in the blanks using the words below to learn more about the important role sand dunes play at the seashore.

adapted	**flooding**	**shelter**
coasts	**sand**	

Sand dune ecosystems on the seashore are important because they store _____________, and they help protect the _____________ further inland from _____________. Plants and animals also make homes in dunes. Dune flora must be _____________ to windy, dry, salty surroundings, so they have long roots to reach groundwater, stems and leaves that hold moisture, and seeds that disperse by wind and water. Burrowing animals are able to dig through the sand and take _____________ in dunes, and they can feed on the vegetation and other animals there.

Color the sand dune and draw any creatures you might expect to see in this ecosystem.

Let's Explore! Create your own sand dune ecosystem in your sandbox or sensory bin. Gather items to represent the plants, animals, and other elements you might find in a sand dune.

047 WHERE ARE THE ZONES IN THE OCEAN?

The open ocean is divided vertically into five major zones based on the characteristics of each section. These zones extend from the ocean's surface to the deepest parts of the sea. Research the ocean zones and what makes each zone unique and distinct from the next.

Color and label the diagram below with the five major zones: epipelagic, mesopelagic, bathypelagic, abyssopelagic, and hadalpelagic.

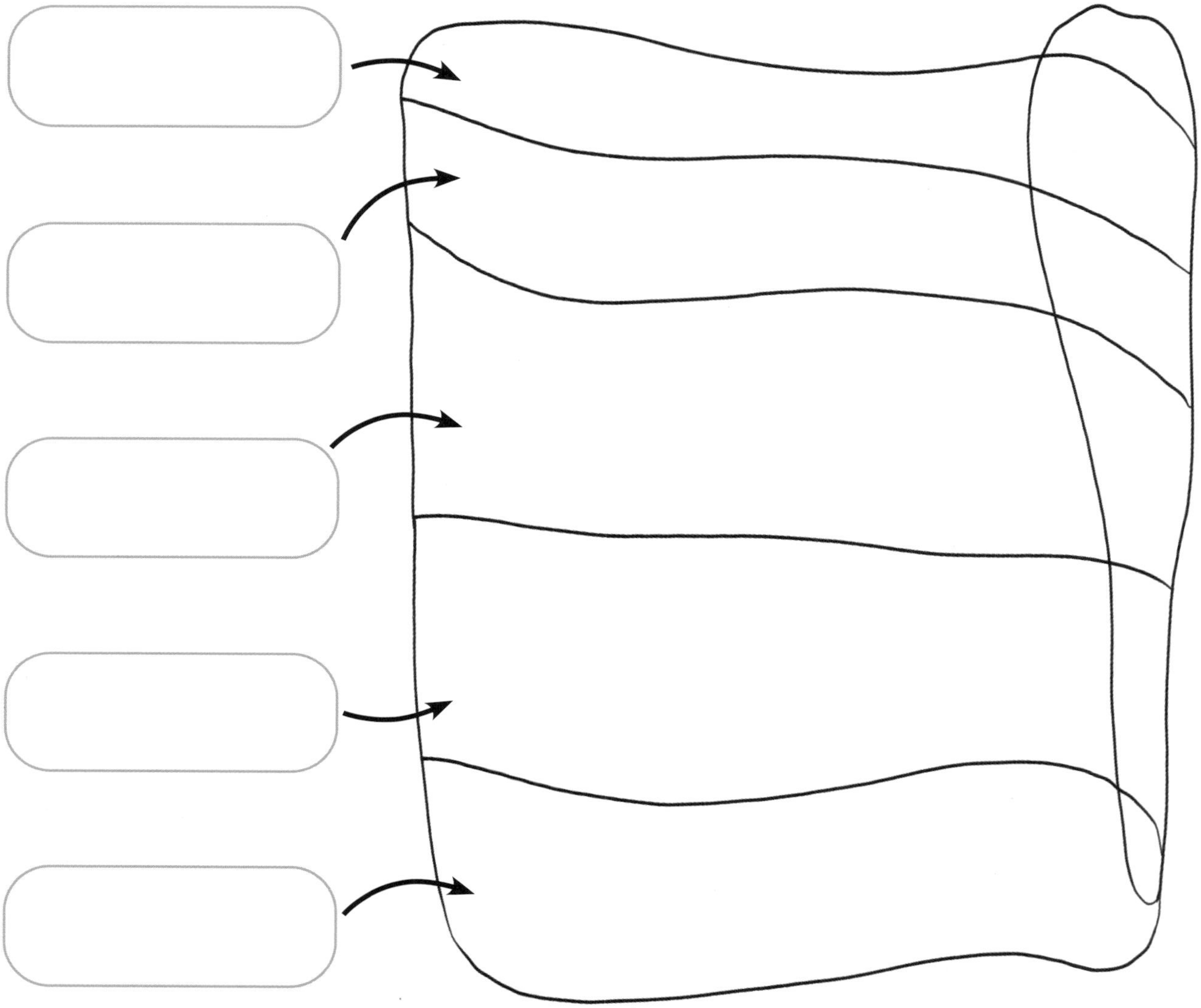

048 WHERE ARE THE WORLD'S OCEANS?

Oceans cover more than two-thirds of Earth's surface! Look at a map or a globe and find Earth's major oceans: Atlantic, Pacific, Arctic, Indian, and Southern. Consider how oceans shape and provide vital resources to the seashore ecosystem.

Can you match ocean-themed vocabulary terms with the correct definition?

biodiversity	area of land next to the ocean
coast	daily rise and fall of the ocean's water caused by the gravitational pull of the Moon and Sun
erosion	Earth's largest and deepest ocean
ocean	energy moving through the water, often caused by wind
Pacific	formed from weathering of rocks and carried and deposited through the process of erosion
sand	large expanse of salt water covering Earth
tide	the carrying away of sediment
wave	the variety of living things living in an area

049 WHY DOES THE TIDE COME IN?

Fill in the blanks using the words below to learn more about the ocean's tides.

beach	**tide**	**waves**
Moon	**twice**	

The ocean's waters move constantly. If you have ever visited the ____________, you probably noticed the ____________ crashing onto the shore. You likely also noticed the water level moving toward you or away from you throughout the day. The ____________ is the movement of water inland and then back out. ____________ each day, seashores experience high tides and low tides. Even though it's far away, the ____________ influences the tides on Earth!

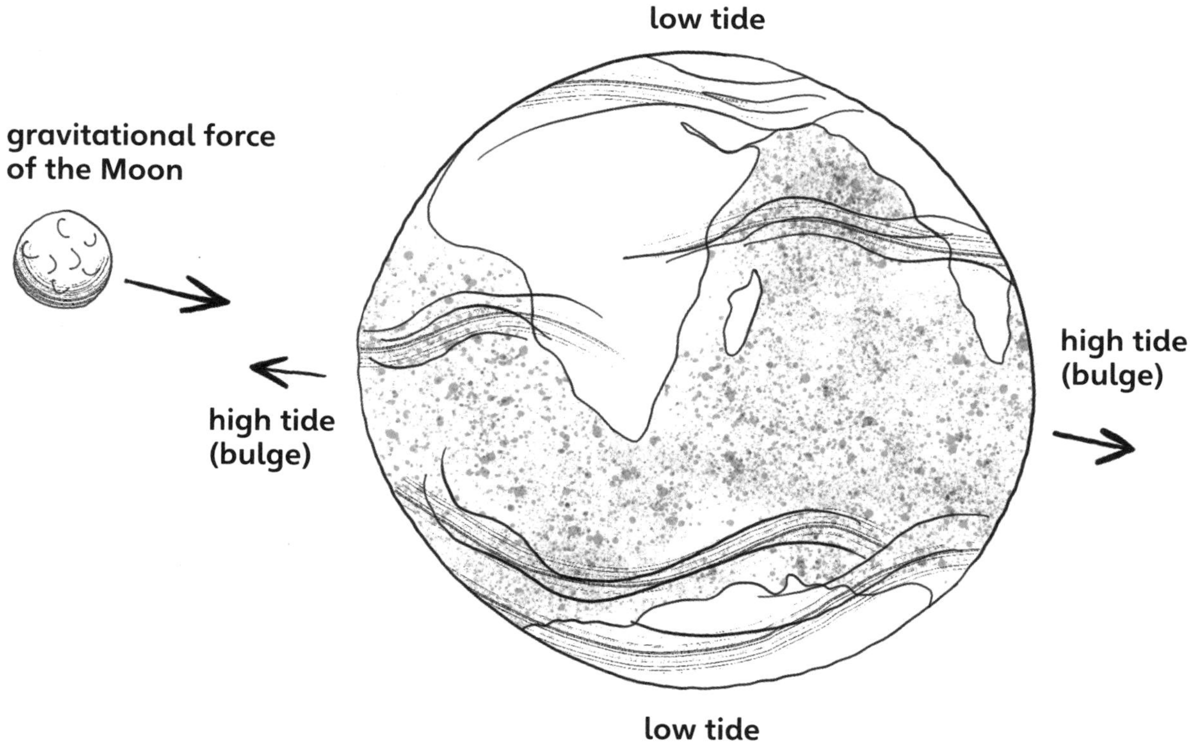

Did You Know? When the Earth, Moon, and Sun are all in a line, tides are higher than normal as the gravitational pull of each is great on Earth's oceans. This alignment is called a spring tide. When the position of the Sun and Moon form a right angle together with the Earth, their pulls work against each other, causing lower than normal tides. This is called a neap tide.

050 WHO RESIDES IN THE TIDES?

Tide pools form as the tide comes in and begins to fill up crevices and depressions in the seashore with water. These pools are home to a diverse range of species and are ecosystems within an ecosystem.

Many animals make their homes in the intertidal zone between the high- and low-tide points. Plankton as well as plant and animal matter come in with the tide, and animals like sea stars, anemones, birds, and barnacles are able to enjoy a meal. These creatures rely on water during high tide and experience dry periods as the tide goes out.

Can you spot the differences in the two tide pools pictured below?

Let's Explore! Create your own mini tide pool in a container with sand, shells, rocks, water, and toy figurines to represent the plant and animal life found in this habitat.

051 ARE SEASHELLS REALLY SHELTERS?

Mollusks make their portable homes out of minerals and proteins. They have an outer layer on their soft bodies called the mantle that makes the three-layered shell and connects the mollusk to it.

Do you have any seashells that match the ones pictured below?

Let's Explore! Try to identify the seashells in your collection. What type of shells are there? What animals did the shells belong to? It might help to find a seashell guide specific to the region where you collected your shells.

cockle

cone

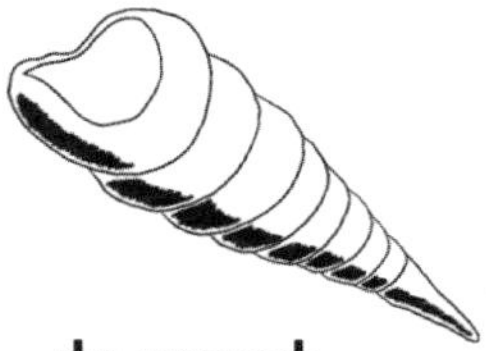

turret

auger

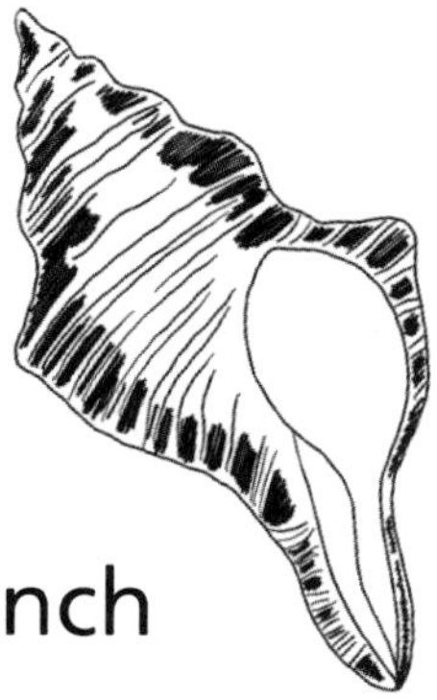

conch

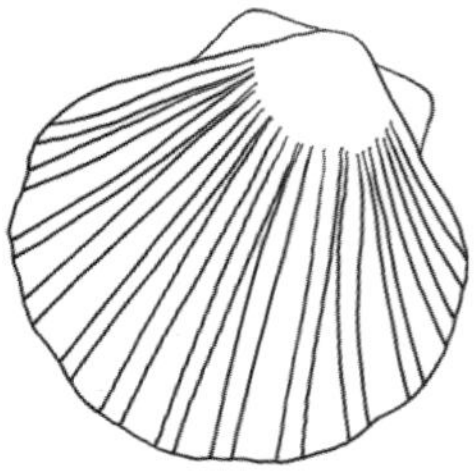

scallop

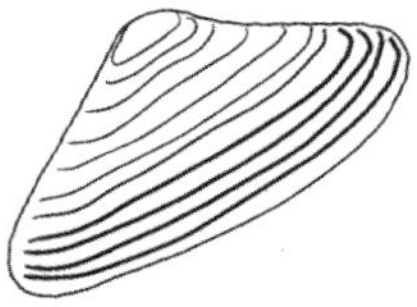

clam

052 WHY DO HERMIT CRABS LIVE IN BORROWED SHELLS?

Hermit crabs are covered with a hard exoskeleton, but their abdomen is soft, hence the need for a shell to cover the abdomen. They search for discarded shells of mollusks to move into so their bodies are protected.

Hermit crabs are scavengers of plant and animal matter, and they make their homes on rocky seashores as well as other beaches. Most live in the ocean, although a few species are terrestrial as adults. Hermit crabs breathe through gills that must stay moist in order to exchange oxygen with the surrounding air.

Use what you learned from the information on hermit crabs to complete the sentences.

exoskeleton **gills** **mollusks** **seashores**

Hermit crabs are covered with a hard ________________.

They use the discarded shells of ________________ to protect their soft abdomens.

Hermit crabs breathe through ________________.

They make their homes on rocky ________________.

053 WHO SPENDS TIME ON THE SEASHORE?

Sea turtles spend most of their lives swimming and drifting with the ocean currents. Adult female sea turtles do visit the seashore each year for an important reason: They lay their eggs on sandy beaches!

Help the sea turtle find her way to shore to lay eggs.

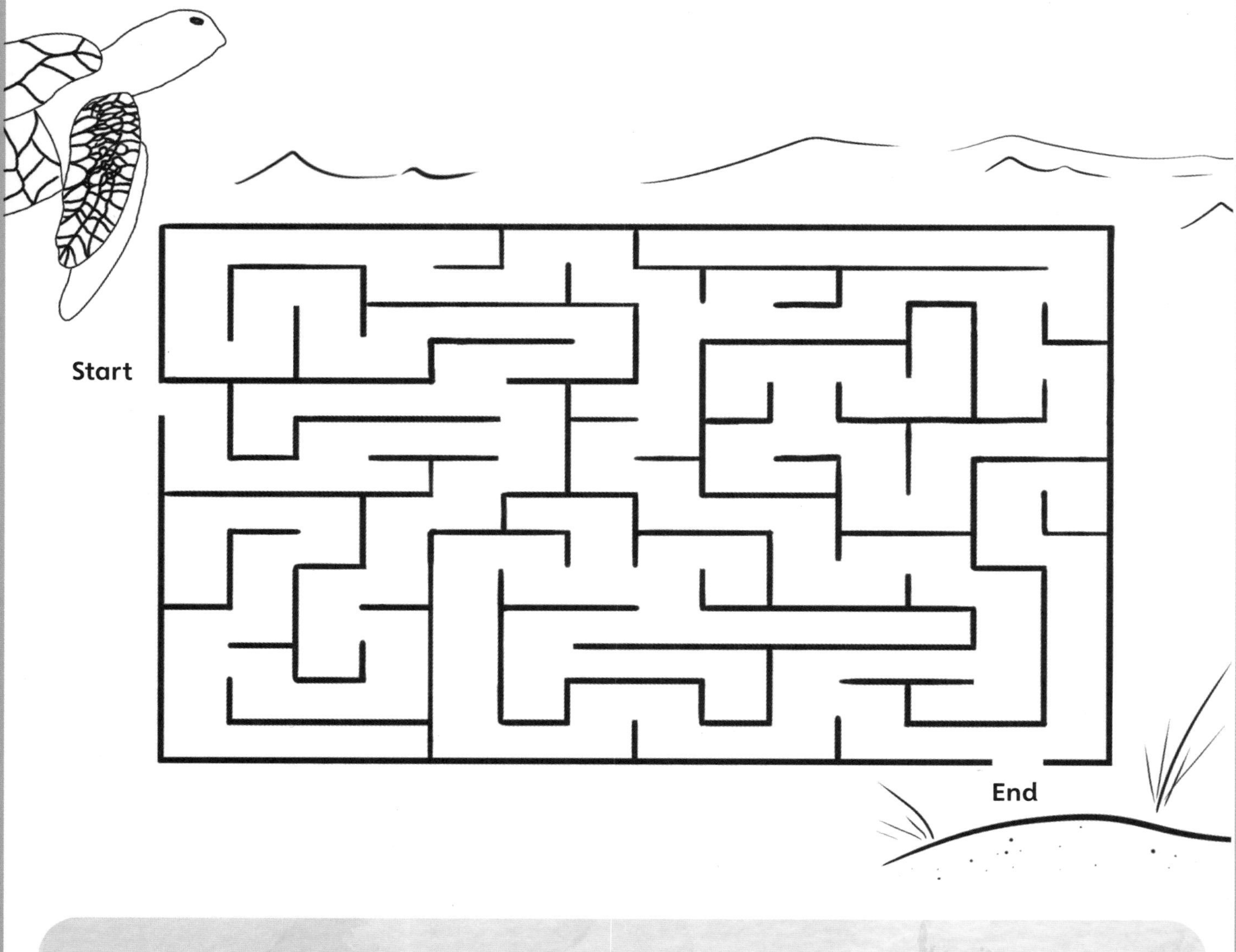

Let's Explore! What turtle species are native to the region where you live? Are they aquatic like sea turtles, or do they live most of their lives on land?

054 WHY IS THE COMMON OCTOPUS EXTRAORDINARY?

Octopuses are found swimming deep in the ocean, hanging out near the coasts, or inhabiting tide pools. Octopuses may even be seen out of the water, crawling around the seashore, looking for food.

Color and label the octopus using the words below.

arm: one of eight limbs, sometimes called tentacles

eye: used to see, thought to be short sighted

head: contains the brain, and arms extend from it

mantle: sac that sits behind the head and holds organs

siphon: funnel-like hole on the side of the mantle used for breathing, propulsion, eliminating waste

sucker: suction cups located along the arms to help with locomotion, grasping, and sensory input

055 HOW DO FISH FORM?

Although the life cycle of fish differs by species, you'll find an example below of how the mahi-mahi goes from a tiny egg to a fully grown fish.

Read the facts about the fish life cycle, color the pictures, and write the correct number next to each stage.

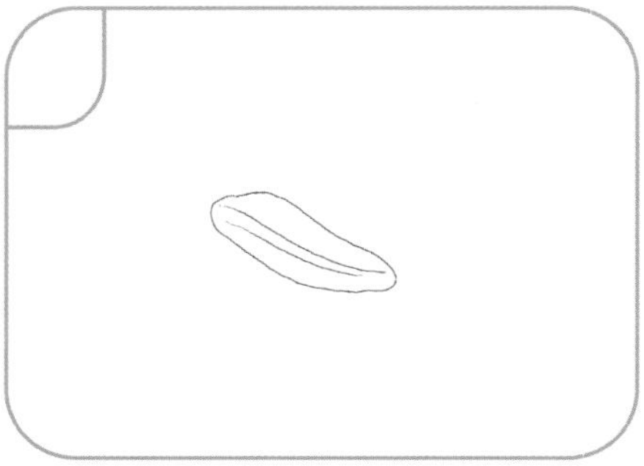

A fish's life begins as a tiny egg.

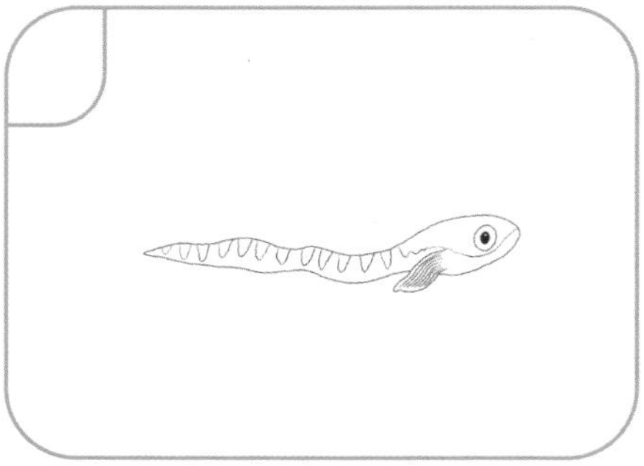

When larval fish begin finding their own food, they are called fry.

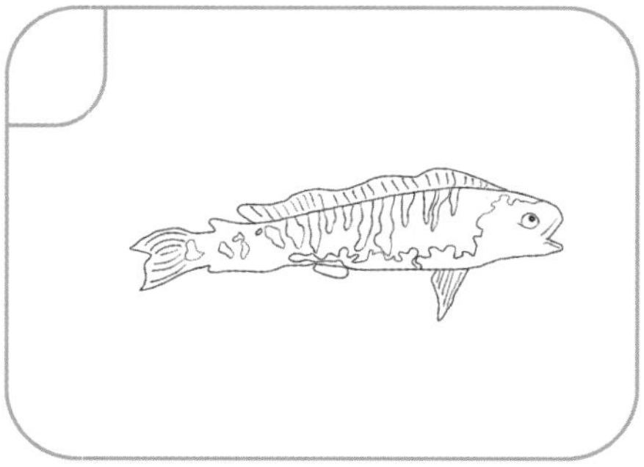

From fry, they become juveniles that get bigger, developing scales and fins as they grow.

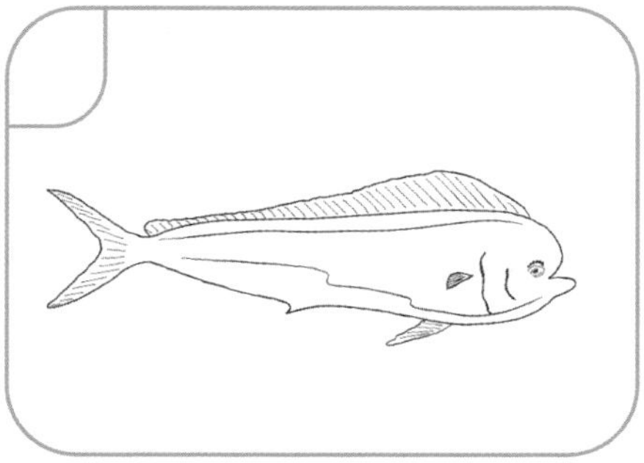

Fish are considered adults when they are fully grown and are able to start the life cycle process all over again.

1. roe (eggs)	**2. fry**	**3. juvenile**	**4. adult mahi-mahi fish**

056 WHY ARE SHARK TEETH SPECIAL?

Sharks may go through up to 30,000 teeth in their lifetime! Shark teeth are among some of the most common fossils found in the world. Take some time to examine the shark teeth in your fossil collection. What do you notice about these teeth? Do they have serrated edges or sharp points and edges?

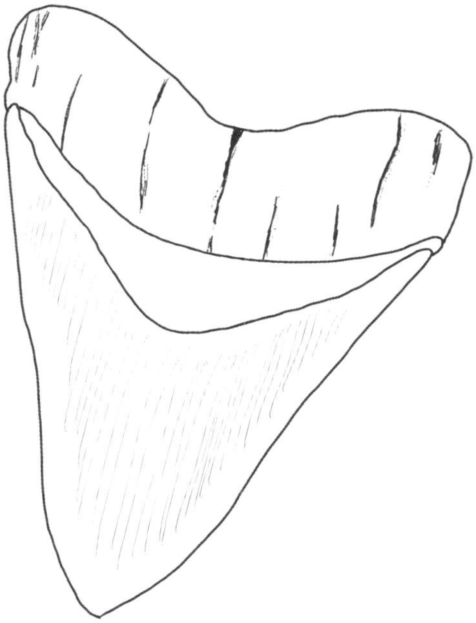

Which statements are true about sharks?

T or F Apex predators such as sharks help keep the ocean ecosystem in balance.

T or F All sharks have large, pointy teeth.

T or F Sharks may lose thousands of teeth over their lifetime.

T or F A shark's teeth help them grasp and eat their prey.

T or F The largest species of sharks have the largest teeth.

057 WHO'S AFRAID OF THE BIG OL' FISH?

Top predators, called apex predators, in the ocean include fish such as sharks, tuna, and billfish like marlin and swordfish. By eating sick or weak animals, predators help keep prey populations healthy and strong. And because predators keep the number of prey animals from growing out of control, they ensure plant populations remain steady.

Create your own seashore food chain by drawing your favorite ocean predator along with its prey. Don't forget to include what the prey animal eats and so on, all the way to plants and the Sun. Describe each link in the chain.

058 MAMMALS OR FISH?

Marine mammals live in coastal regions around the world, spending part or all their lives in the sea.

All mammals have hair on their bodies at some stage of their lives, breathe air through lungs, and make milk to feed their babies. And unlike most fish and other marine creatures, marine mammals are warm-blooded (endothermic), meaning they maintain a constant body temperature.

Fish are also vertebrates, so they have skeletons of bone or cartilage. Instead of taking air into their lungs, they usually use gills to get the oxygen they need. Fish are often covered in scales rather than skin and fur like mammals, and most are cold-blooded (ectothermic), meaning their body temperature depends on their surroundings.

Using the above information and your own research, fill in the T-chart to compare and contrast the characteristics of marine mammals and fish.

Marine Mammals	Fish

059 WHERE ARE THE WHALES?

Spotting cetaceans, such as whales, dolphins, or porpoises, can be a challenge when on shore, but if you know what to look for, your chances of seeing them improve dramatically. While surveying the scene, watch for **spouts** going upward. Different-shaped spouts suggest different species. The same principle applies to **dorsal fins** and **flukes**. You might get a peek at these emerging from the water. Their sizes and colors vary depending on the species. Large splashes in the water may also indicate a whale has **breached**, and smaller splashes may mean a pod of dolphins is offshore.

Use the hints to help you identify the whale-watching terms.

Hint: These form when whales and dolphins breathe out warm air that condenses and creates water droplets in the air.

____

Hint: Large splashes in the water may also indicate a whale has done this.

____

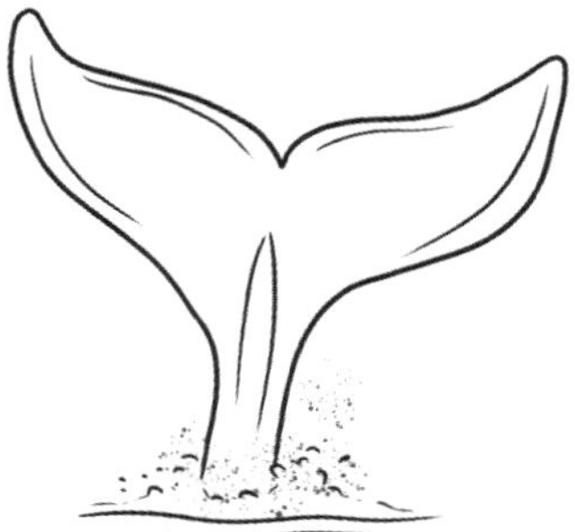

Hint: A whale might expose this as they angle themselves to thrust into deeper waters.

____

Hint: This sits on the top of a whale's back and is noticeable when a whale grazes the ocean's surface.

____

060 WHICH BEAK IS BEST?

Most birds use their beaks to both grasp and eat their food, so the shapes and features of their beaks are adapted for specific diets. Whatever the meal, there's a bird beak adapted to eat it!

Take a look at the different bird beaks. Match each picture with the correct beak type and description.

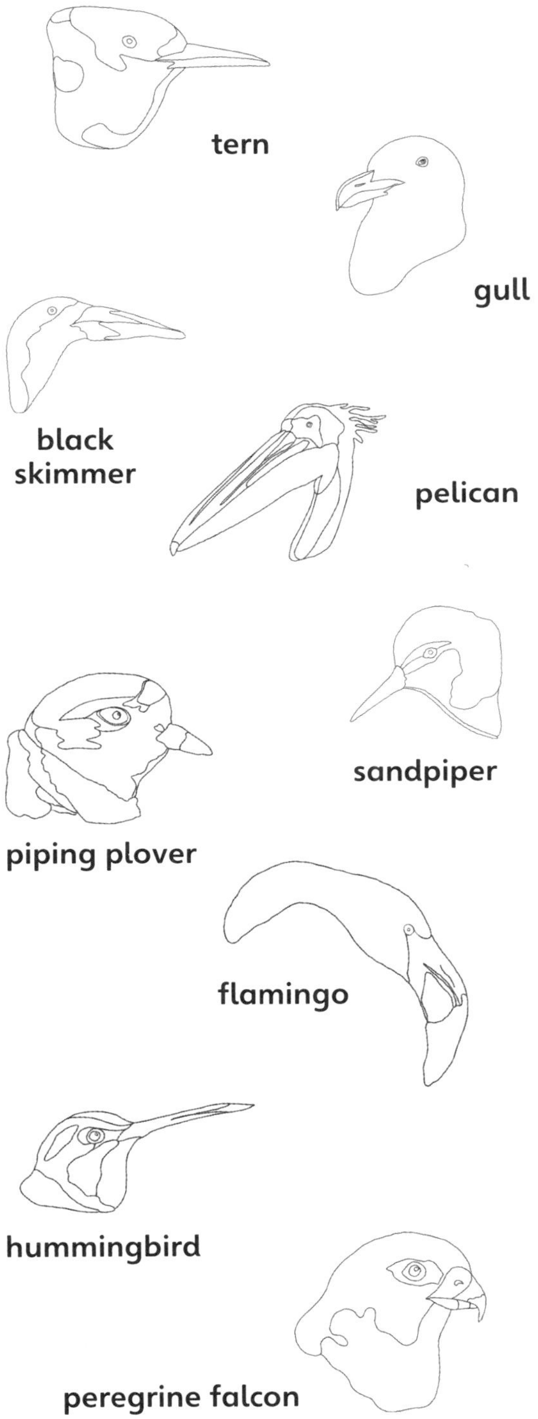

dip netting: expandable lower beak for scooping fish

filter feeding: large beak with a filter system for removing food from water

fishing: long, strong, pointed beak for grabbing fish

generalist: relatively large, curved upper mandible for eating a variety of foods

insect eating: narrow beak, like tweezers, for grabbing invertebrates

mud probing: slim beak to dig for buried invertebrates

nectar feeding: long, thin beak to reach into flowers for nectar

raptorial: sharp, hooked beak for tearing prey

surface skimming: longer lower beak to scoop up fish from the water's surface

061 HOW DO BIRDS SURVIVE ON THE SEASHORE?

Fill in the blanks using the words below to learn more about shorebird adaptations.

adaptations	**invertebrates**	**niches**	**seashore**

Around 200 species of birds make the __________________ their home, including pelicans, plovers, and gulls. Birds at the seashore fill different __________________ to avoid competing with each other for food in their coastal ecosystem. They share common characteristics and also have __________________ unique to their species.

Gulls are vital to the food webs in their seashore ecosystems. The herring gull is usually what you picture when you think "gull." Herring gulls feed from both land and sea, eating fish and __________________.

062 WHAT'S SPECIAL ABOUT THE SEASHORE?

Visit the seashore or any body of water for inspiration. Pay close attention to the water, the shoreline, the plants, and the animals that live there. What is the composition of the coast? Is it rocky, sandy, muddy, or maybe a combination? Illustrate the images you see or take photos to use in your nature journal. Focus on the entire ecosystem or a single species as you create your nature journal entry.

063 SEASHORE QUIZ

Test your knowledge by answering these questions using the word bank below.

1. This ecosystem is found where the ocean biome meets the land. ____________
2. What may form when grasses and shrubs trap blowing sands on the beach? ____________
3. These are formed by weathering, erosion, and waves crashing along the coast. ____________
4. This forms when rocks, seashells, and other materials are worn into tiny particles. ____________
5. What is the term for the vertical divisions of the ocean? ____________
6. What is the world's largest biome? ____________
7. These occur as energy travels through the ocean, often caused by wind. ____________
8. Many make their homes in this area between high and low tide. ____________
9. What is the term for when the water level moves inland and then back out? ____________
10. What celestial object's gravitational force influences the world's oceans, causing the tides?

    ____
11. This seashore ecosystem forms as the tide comes in and empties as the tide goes out.

    ____
12. These mollusk exoskeletons are made up of minerals and proteins. ____________
13. What creatures visit the seashore to lay eggs on the sandy beaches? ____________
14. These creatures squirt ink to distract predators while they make their escape. ____________
15. These apex predators help keep the ocean ecosystem in balance. ____________
16. What type of vertebrates have gills, are covered in scales, and are cold-blooded? ____________
17. These mammals live all or part of their lives in the sea. ____________
18. One way to identify a whale is by looking at this structure on its back. ____________
19. This bird species eats both fish and invertebrates near the shore. ____________
20. Part of a bird that's adapted for its specific diet. ____________

beak	gull	octopuses	sharks
coastal landforms	intertidal zone	sand	the ocean
dorsal fin	marine mammals	sea turtles	tide
dunes	Moon	seashells	tide pool
fish	ocean zones	seashore	waves

4

GRASSLANDS

Discover!

DISCOVER!

Grasslands are found throughout the world and on every continent with the exception of Antarctica. Receiving less rain than forests but more than deserts, prairies and savannas are known for their abundance of grasses and sparse tree growth. Animals are adapted to life in the open plains with colors and patterns to camouflage them against the tall grass. **Camouflage** allows creatures to blend into their surroundings and sneak up on prey or hide from predators.

Herbivores are plentiful in the prairies and savannas around the world. With lots of vegetation to feed on, they often group together in herds for safety in the wide expanses of their ecosystems. Grazing stimulates grass growth, and animal hooves dig into the soil, making space for seeds to germinate. Grazers help prevent woody vegetation from growing in grasslands, so grasses don't have to compete with trees for resources such as sunlight and water.

Wildfires also prevent tree growth in grasslands. Lightning is a natural firestarter, and fire helps clear the ground of woody vegetation and dead plants, opening areas for new grasses to start fresh. Ash left behind from fires provides nutrients, and the newly bare soil is warmed by the Sun. While animals can escape wildfires by flying, running, and burrowing, plants are unable to move. Growth points near the ground, or even underground, allow grasses to continue to grow even after quick-burning fires move through the region.

Words from the Wild

Wildfire: uncontrolled, natural fire burning in the wilderness

Camouflage: color or pattern that allows an animal to blend into its surroundings

Carbon cycle: process of carbon moving through the environment between the atmosphere, plants, animals, and the soil

Seed dispersal: plant's method of spreading seeds to new areas for germination

Burrow: an underground shelter, whether tunnel or den, created by an animal

064 WHO LIVES IN THE GRASSLANDS?

Grasslands provide a habitat for many creatures, from tiny insects to huge elephants. Herbivores feed on the abundant species of grasses and wildflowers, and carnivores act as predators, feeding on the herbivores. Grasslands, such as temperate prairies and tropical savannas, benefit the natural world and all its inhabitants.

Can you match the animal and plant species to their grassland habitat?

North American Prairie

African Savanna

bison

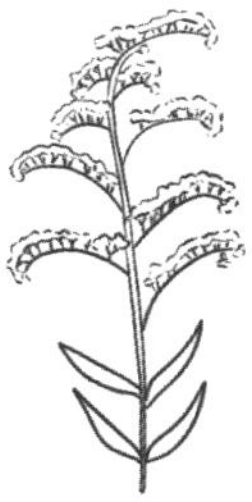

goldenrod

prairie dog

baboon

lion

elephant grass

wildebeest

bobcat

065 HOW DO FIRES HELP GRASSLANDS FLOURISH?

Wildfires sound scary and destructive, but they have a purpose, and grassland plants and animals have adaptations for surviving these powerful natural events. In fact, grasslands rely on fire to keep woody plants from growing and taking over the ecosystem.

Which statements are true about grassland fires?

T or F Wildfires usually happen during the dry season.

T or F Animals in the grassland may escape wildfires with their speed or by burrowing underground.

T or F The roots and underground stems of grasses can no longer grow after a wildfire.

T or F Wildfires help keep woody plants and trees from taking over a grassland.

T or F Grassland wildfires are only destructive and serve no purpose.

Did You Know? When a passing fire clears plant litter, the soil is able to warm up in the Sun, and soil microbes become more active as they break down decaying roots and other plant material to add nutrients to the soil.

066 WHAT CAUSES TWIRLING TORNADOES?

Dangerous storms and even tornadoes occasionally develop over the vast, open stretches of grassland. When cold and warm air masses meet, violent rainstorms with lightning and tornadoes can be the result. Swirling funnels may form when the warm air currents rise upward as cold air travels downward.

Color and label the aspects of tornado development with the corresponding number from the diagram.

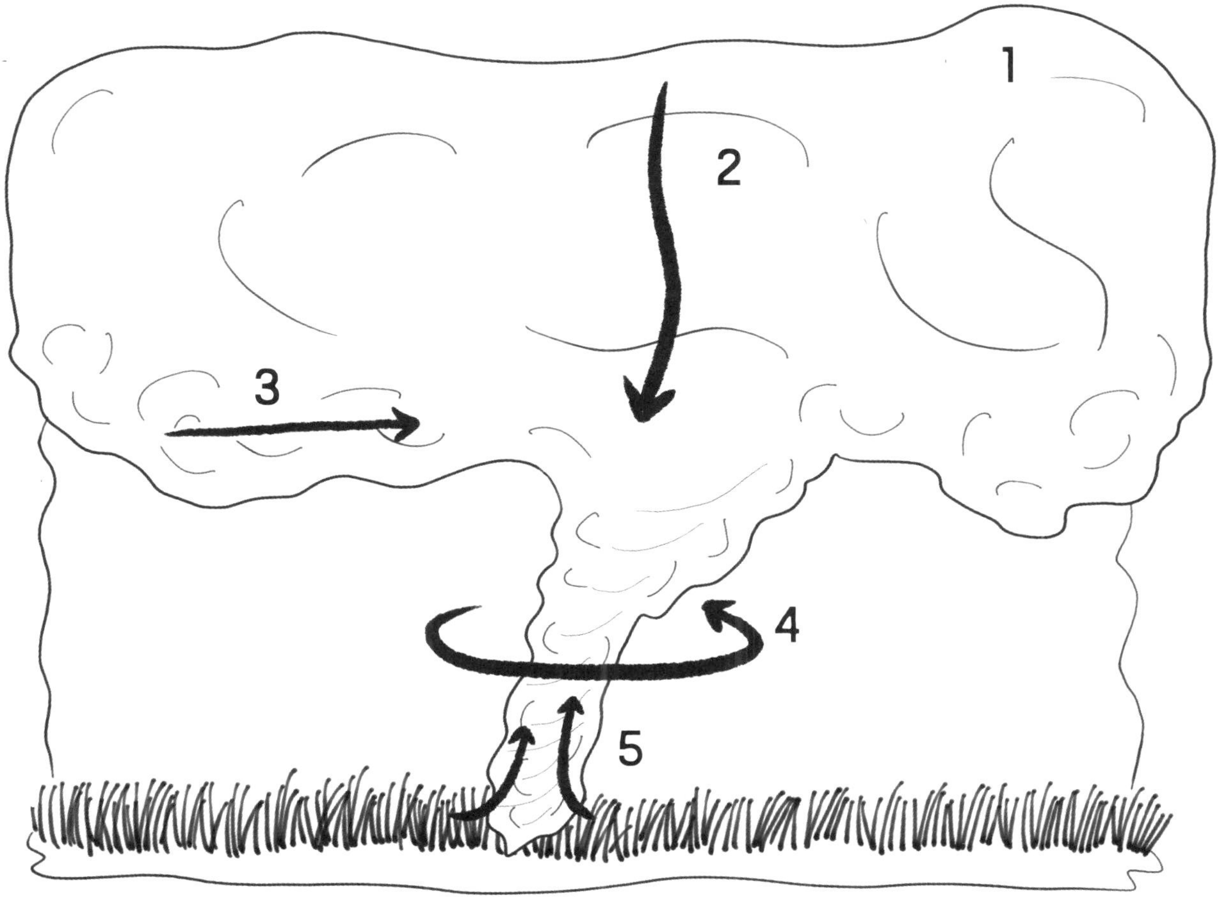

_______ cold air pushes down, feeds into tunnel formation

_______ cumulonimbus cloud

_______ horizontal wind shear begins circulation

_______ warm, humid air rises

_______ winds form counterclockwise rotation

067 WHAT ARE THE PARTS OF POACEAE?

Poaceae, commonly known as grasses, are adapted to life with grazing animals and wildfires because they have growth points at or below ground level. These are not likely to be eaten by grazers or destroyed by fire. Prairie plants may also have rhizomes underground from which new shoots grow upward.

Color and label the grass using the words below.

crown: where grass growth starts, just above the roots

culm: the above-ground stem

inflorescence: the flower head, contains the spikelets

leaf blade: extends from the culm, responsible for photosynthesis

node: where a new leaf grows

roots: below the surface of the soil, these take in water and nutrients

sheath: surrounds the culm at the base of the plant

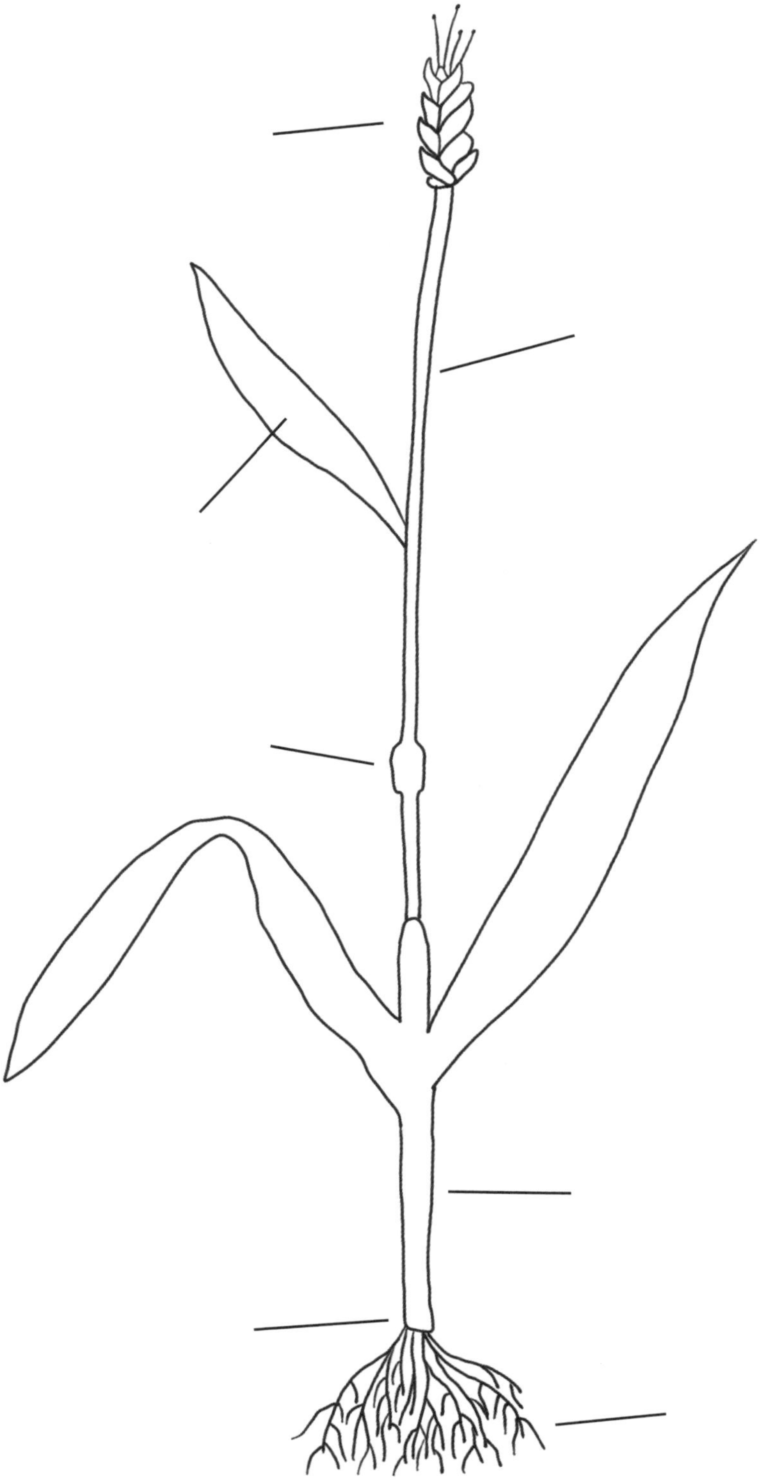

068 HOW DOES CARBON GO THROUGH A GRASSLAND?

Grassland soils are a storehouse for a huge amount of Earth's carbon. The rich soils keep the grassland alive by providing nutrients for new plants to grow. This process is part of the carbon cycle, where carbon is moved from the atmosphere to living things that eventually decay, break down, and release carbon into their surroundings.

Color and study the carbon cycle diagram, then answer the questions below.

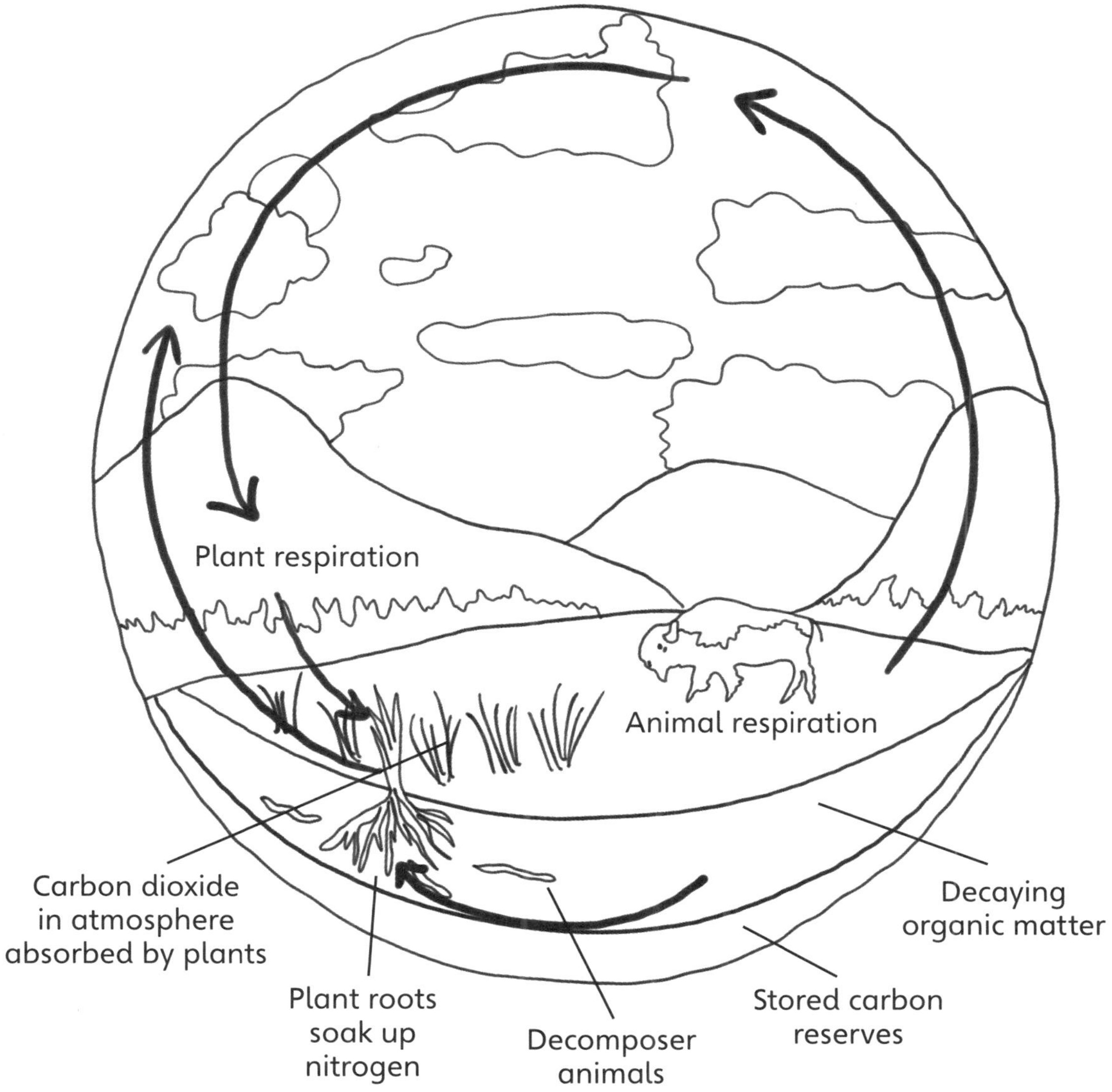

What gas in the atmosphere contains carbon? ______________________________

Why do grasses need carbon from the atmosphere? ______________________________

Where do grasses store excess carbon? ______________________________

069 HOW DO SEEDS SCATTER IN GRASSLANDS?

When seeds land on the ground and have good soil, water, sunlight, and space to grow, they have the chance to reproduce. Plants have different methods for dispersing their seeds, so they can grow in new areas.

Match the plants with the correct seed type by drawing a line between the picture and seed dispersal method.

Sunflower: produces seeds in the center of the flower, and many sunflower seeds are consumed and dispersed by birds.

Willow: uses wind to disperse its seeds. The fluffy part of the seed helps the wind carry the seed away from the parent plant.

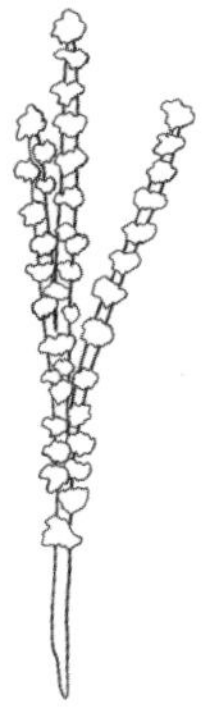

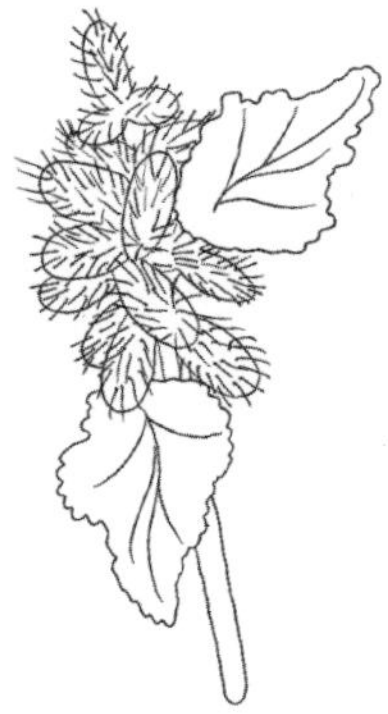

Cocklebur: has prickly seeds that can stick to fur and be dispersed by animals. The seeds are also able to float and can be dispersed by water.

Lupine: ejects its seeds from dried seed pods through ballistic dispersal, and the seeds land several feet from the parent plant.

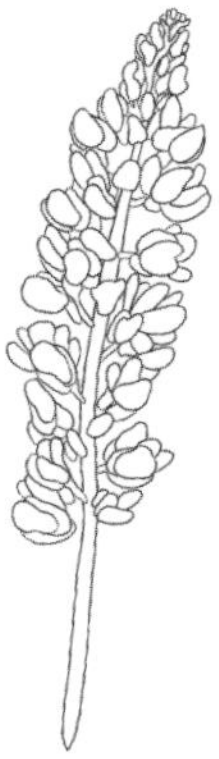

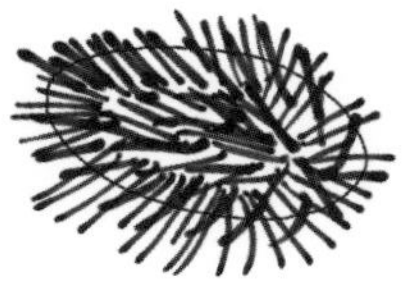

stick to fur

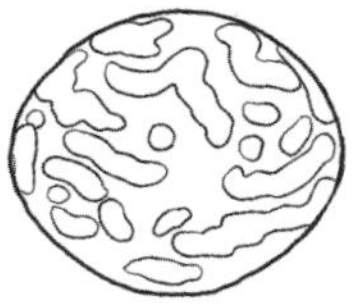

ballistic

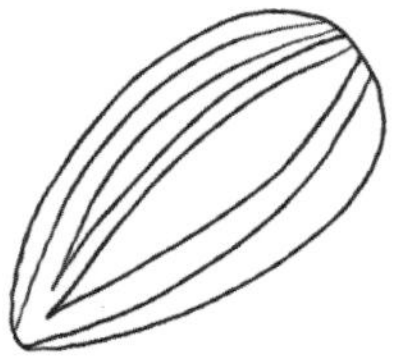

food for animals that spread seeds in scat

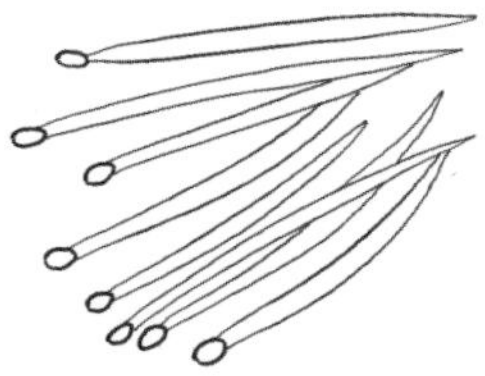

wind

Did You Know? Sunflowers grow up to 10 feet (3 m) tall and bloom from summer into fall. Their seeds are eaten by several animal species including mammals, insects, and birds.

070 HOW DO GRASSLAND PLANTS ADAPT?

Grasses may define the grassland ecosystem, but they are not the only plants living in grasslands. Forbs and sparse trees are also found in grasslands.

Can you go out in nature and find plants with adaptations similar to the ones below?

Coneflowers are able to survive hot, dry prairie summers and have long roots to reach water underground.

Bermuda grass grows well in open sunlight and can withstand drought and wildfires.

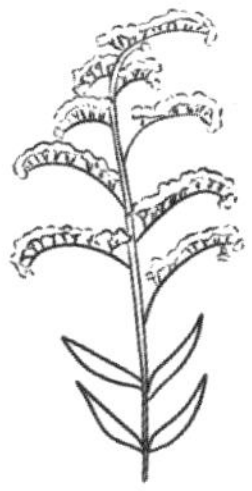

Goldenrod is pollinated by bees and butterflies in grasslands, and its seeds are dispersed by the powerful prairie winds.

Elephant grass grows tall in the savanna and has sharp leaf blades and shallow roots to absorb water quickly after it rains.

Prairie sunflowers thrive in prairies with broad leaves to absorb sunlight and scratchy stems to protect them from hungry herbivores.

071 WHO RULES THE GRASSLANDS?

Grasslands around the world are home to a variety of animals that eat meat or vegetation or sometimes both. Based on the common characteristics of carnivores (eat meat), herbivores (eat plants), and omnivores (eat both), categorize the following grassland animals based on which foods they likely eat.

African wild dog	**cheetah**	**giraffe**	**pronghorn**
baboon	**coyote**	**kangaroo**	**tortoise**
bison	**eagle**	**lion**	**wildebeest**
bobcat	**elephant**	**prairie dog**	**zebra**

Carnivore	Herbivore	Omnivore

072 WHAT'S UNDERGROUND IN THE GRASSLAND?

Animals living in grasslands must have adaptations to survive in a wide-open area where there are few hiding places and where weather can be extreme. Not only do animals such as prairie dogs stay hidden from predators underground, they are protected from weather and wildfires as well.

Can you help the prairie dog find its way through the burrow?

Let's Explore! You can make a burrow for yourself using items you have at home like pillows, cushions, sheets, and blankets.

073 CAN YOU CREATE A GRASSLAND FOOD CHAIN?

Predators in the grassland biome, like any other biome, are vital to the individual ecosystems. Predators keep rodent populations under control, herbivore herds healthy, and plant communities from being overgrazed or overgrown. Too many herbivores can lead to a loss of plant communities.

Create your own grassland food chain by drawing your favorite grassland predator along with its prey. Don't forget to include what the prey animal eats and so on, all the way to plants and the Sun. Describe each link in the chain.

Did You Know? When plants disappear from the ecosystem, food sources disappear with them, along with cover for smaller species that hide among the grasses and forbs.

074 WHO'S HIDING IN THE GRASSLANDS?

Camouflage gives grassland predators an advantage when catching their prey. For example, tigers and cheetahs have stripes and spots to break up their outline in tall grasses, while lions and coyotes are similarly colored to their surroundings, making them hard to see.

Let's Explore! Go on a nature walk to look for animals with good camouflage. Familiarize yourself ahead of time with animals you might see while you're out and about so you know where to look and what to look for. Report on what you found below. Draw the different animals you saw and describe how they used camouflage to blend in with the surroundings.

075 HOW DO GRASSLAND BIRDS GROW?

Birds are well-known for laying eggs in all different sizes and colors depending on the species. This is how birds reproduce to ensure survival of their species.

Read the facts about the bird life cycle. Color and label each by writing the correct number next to each stage.

1. egg **2. chick** **3. adult**

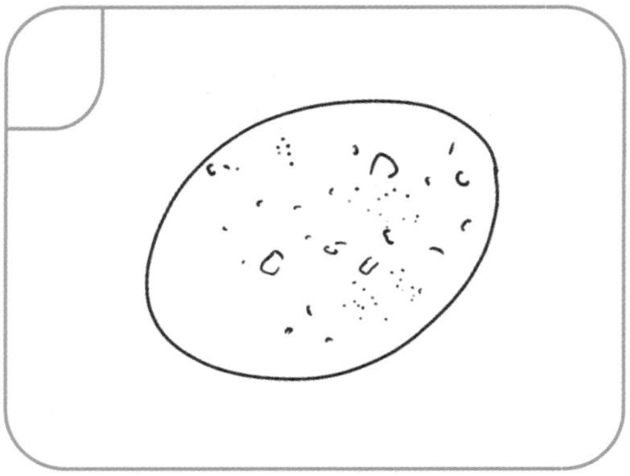

The cycle starts with the laying of a fertilized egg, which is incubated by one or both parents.

When a baby chick first hatches, it's called a hatchling, then a nestling, and finally a fledgling.

Soon the chicks will be adults that are able to reproduce and raise chicks of their own.

076 WHERE DO GRASSLAND BIRDS MAKE THEIR HOMES?

Without an abundance of trees, you might think grassland bird species would be few. But grasslands make successful habitats for foraging, hunting, and nesting for a variety of species, from small songbirds to migrating waterfowl to powerful raptors. As in any ecosystem, different species have different needs. Some prefer tall grasses, others medium and short grasses. Wherever they make their home, large areas that support habitat needs are important to all species.

Visit a nature center or natural area in a grassland ecosystem if you have one in your region. Alternatively, you could visit a park with a meadow or open field, or read a book about grasslands. Choose a bird species that catches your eye. Draw a picture of it and write about your observations below, paying particular attention to how and where it makes its home.

NAME OF SPECIES:

DRAW THE SPECIES:

DESCRIBE ITS APPEARANCE:

WHAT DOES IT EAT?

WHAT IS ITS HABITAT LIKE?

DESCRIBE THE HOME IT MAKES FOR ITSELF:

077 WHAT TYPES OF FEATHERS ARE FOUND ON GRASSLAND BIRDS?

It's no secret that birds are covered in feathers. In fact, it's one of the characteristics that makes them birds. Feathers are made of a protein called keratin, which is the same protein found in your hair and fingernails. There are several different types of feathers adapted for different functions.

Let's Explore! Color and study the examples of different feather types below. Do you have any feathers in your nature collection that match the feathers pictured? Compare the feathers in the diagram with those you've collected during your nature walks and try to identify the feather type.

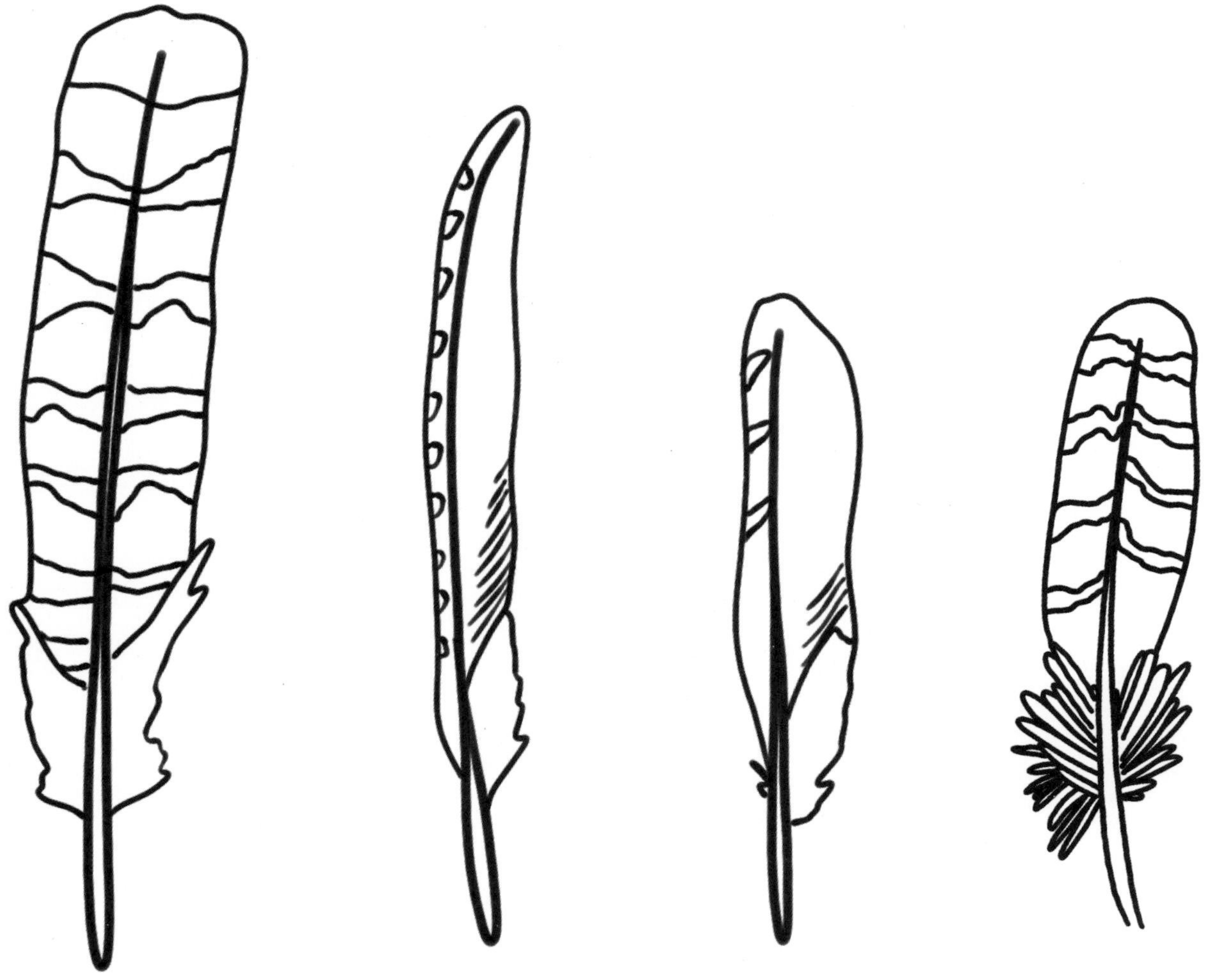

078 WHAT DO YOU KNOW ABOUT THE REPTILE LIFE CYCLE?

Fill in the blanks using the words below to learn more about the reptile life cycle.

crocodilians	**eggs**	**hatchlings**	**parents**	**predators**

Most reptiles hatch from _______________. When babies emerge, they are called _______________. Hatchlings look very similar to their _______________, except for their small size and coloring. Most hatchlings, with the exception of _______________, are on their own without parents to watch over them. Reptile hatchlings have to find their own food and water, and they must learn to hide or defend themselves from _______________.

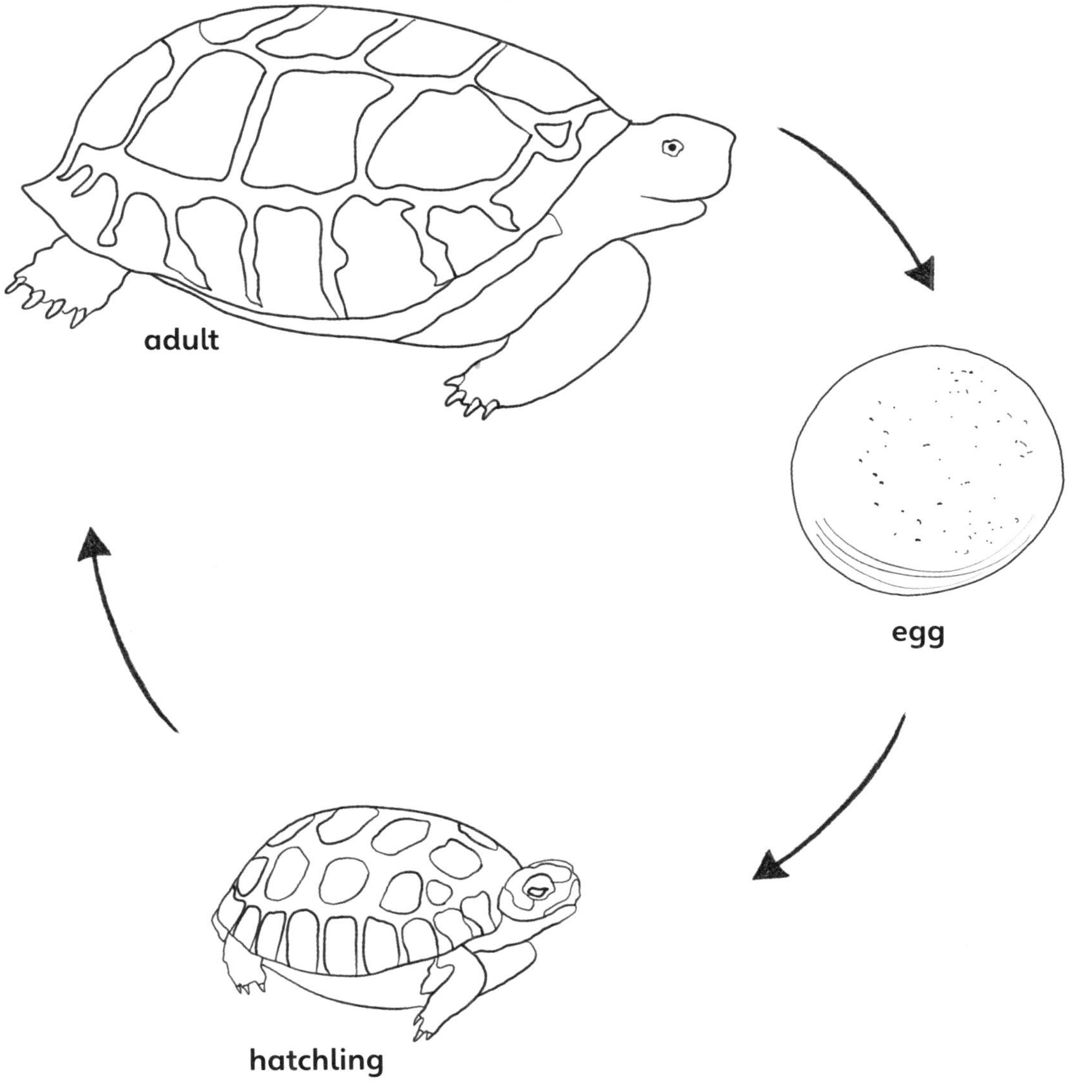

079 HOW DO YOU DRAW A TORTOISE?

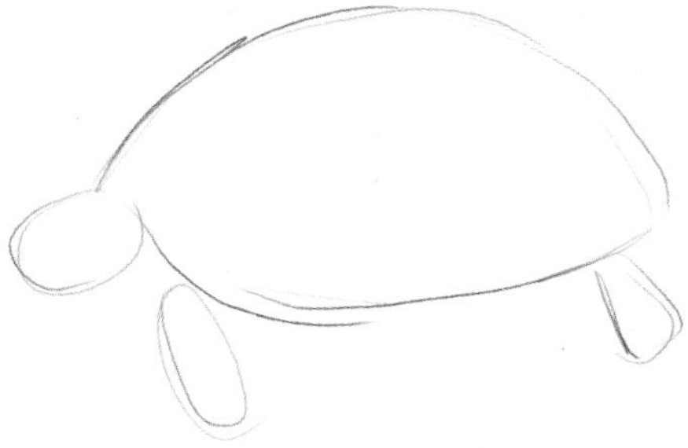

1. Start by sketching out the basic shape of your tortoise.

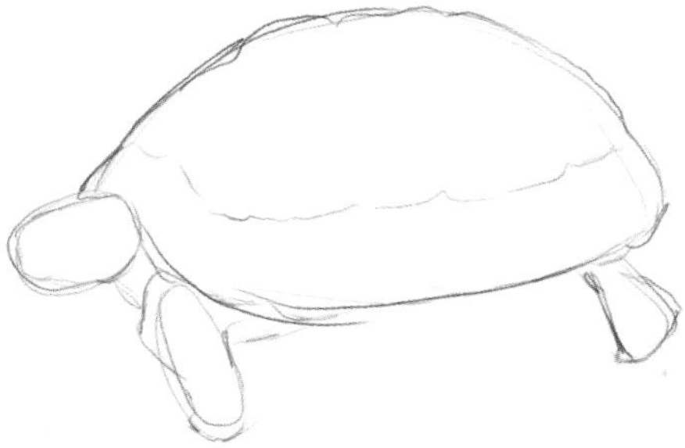

2. Next, add some definition to your tortoise's shell, head, and legs.

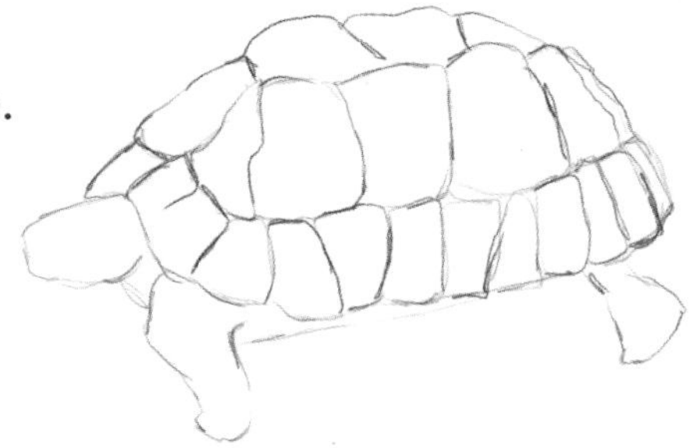

3. Start adding details to your tortoise's shell by drawing the scutes.

4. Add more details such as the eyes, nose, mouth, and scales on the legs.

5. Once you're happy with your tortoise, you can define the lines either by pressing firmly with your pencil or with an ink pen.

YOUR TURN!

Did You Know? Tortoises feed on grasses and forbs in grasslands. They have scales to keep them from drying out and to protect them from predators. Their coloration and markings allow them to blend into their habitat. And they are able to dig, creating burrows underground.

080 WHY ARE CICADAS SPECIAL?

Known for their interesting life cycle, young cicadas dig into the ground where they feed and grow over many years and eventually emerge as adults. The bush cicada lives in the grasslands of North America. During its development, this annual cicada feeds on the juices of grass roots. As adults, the males cling to grasses and make buzzing calls to attract the females.

Color and label the cicada using the words below.

abdomen: final and largest body segment

antennae: pair of sense organs on the head

compound eyes: made up of many separate visual units

head: front most segment

six legs: three pairs of legs for digging and climbing

thorax: middle segment

wings: large with prominent veins

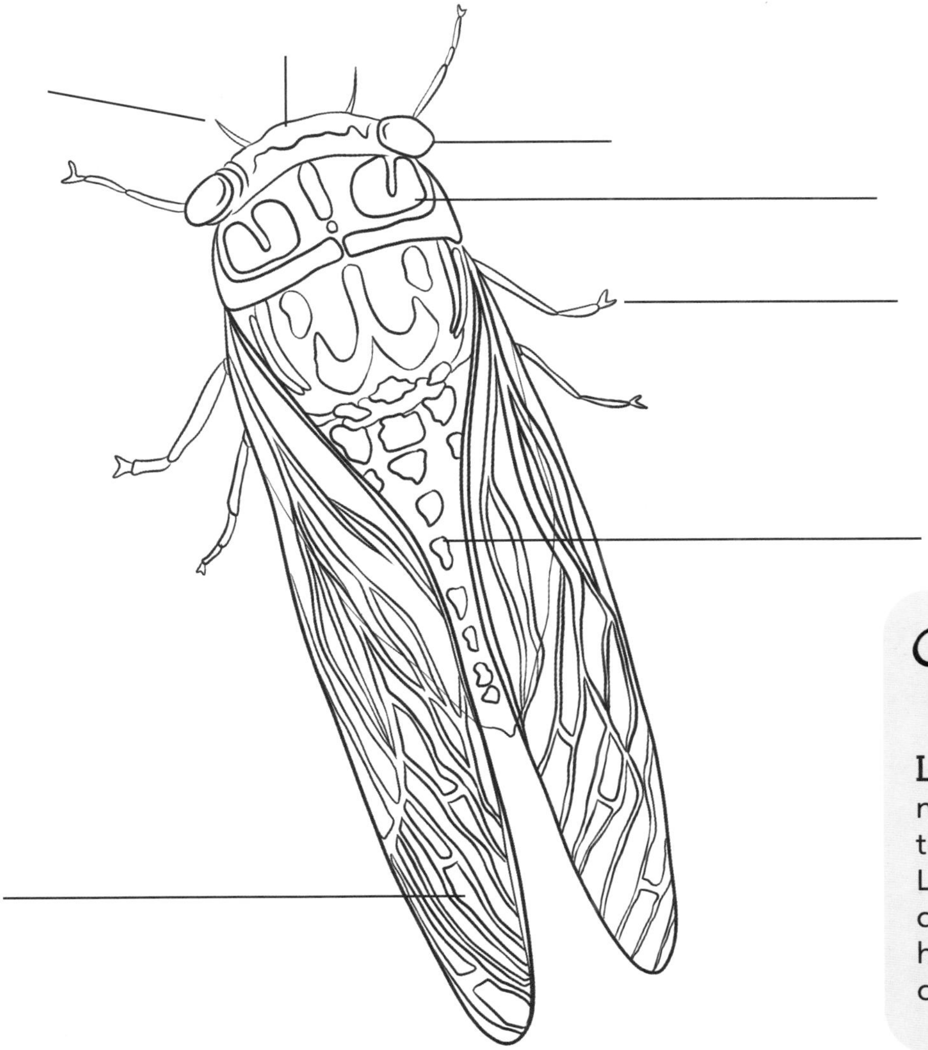

Let's Explore! Go on a nature walk to listen for the cacophony of cicadas. Look on tree trunks for cicada exoskeletons that have been shed so the cicada can develop.

081 CAN YOU IDENTIFY THE INVERTEBRATE?

Greater diversity in plant species attracts more insect species and other invertebrates, so healthy prairies and savannas are teeming with these creatures. Grasslands benefit from having invertebrates inhabiting them. Invertebrates are animals that do not have a backbone or internal skeleton, but they may have an exoskeleton instead.

Circle all the grassland invertebrates in the images below. Place an "X" on those invertebrates that are also insects.

082 WHERE DO TERMITES TREAD IN THE GRASSLANDS?

Fill in the blanks using the words below to learn more about termite mounds.

aerate	**mound**	**pollinate**	**rotting wood**	**savannas**

Termites thrive in African ______________ where they live in burrows or build large ______________ nests above ground. In building their homes, termites help ______________ the soil and allow water to move through. Their mounds, once abandoned, offer shelter to other creatures such as scorpions, ants, and reptiles. Termites also break down ______________ and return its nutrients to the soil. They ______________ certain flower species. And, of course, termites provide food for other animals and people.

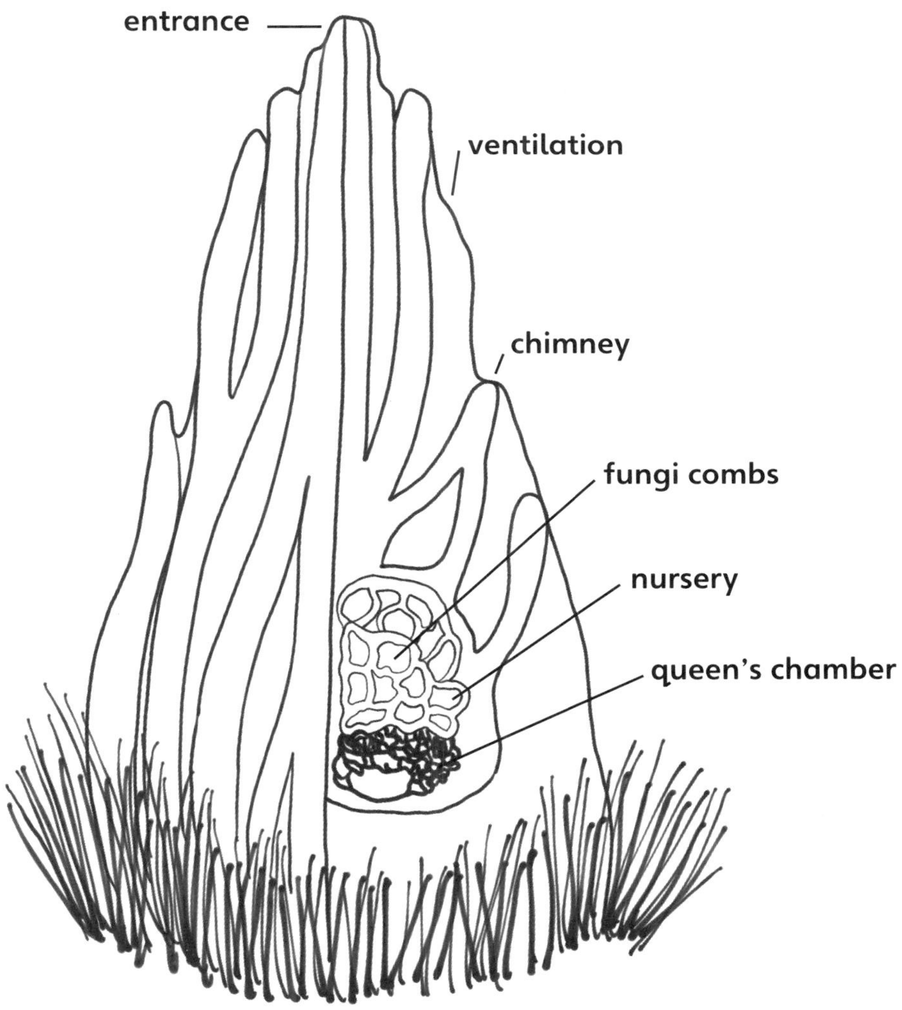

083 WHAT'S GREAT ABOUT GRASSLANDS?

Visit a grassland region such as a prairie or savanna. Observe the tall grasses and forbs. What colors do you notice in this biome? Make note of the different animals you see including their type, size, and color. Try to find species of insects, reptiles, amphibians, birds, and mammals. Which groups are easiest to spot among the grasses?

084 GRASSLAND QUIZ

Test your knowledge by answering these questions using the word bank below.

1. Grasslands are found on all but which continent?
2. Grasslands rely on this natural occurrence to keep woody plants from taking over the ecosystem.
3. These produce a powerful vortex that can destroy everything in its path.
4. This is one of the most abundant types of plants on the planet.
5. What are the horizontal, underground stems from which grasses can grow upward?
6. This chemical element is stored in abundance within grassland soils.
7. What process enables plants to spread seeds away from the parent plant?
8. This tall flower is a food source for many grassland animals.
9. These plants grow few and far between in the grassland ecosystem.
10. What is the term to describe animals that exclusively eat vegetation?
11. What is the underground dwelling that some grassland animals dig called?
12. These animals keep herbivore populations under control and the grassland ecosystem balanced.
13. This speedy grassland predator has spots on its fur to help it blend in.
14. Many animals use this cryptic coloration to hide from or confuse other animals.
15. These animals are well-known for laying eggs and building nests.
16. These coverings are made of keratin and are a distinct characteristic of birds.
17. What type of animal looks very similar to their parents when they hatch?
18. What grassland residents are covered with scales and a hard shell to protect them from predators?
19. Attracted by the diversity in plant species, these creatures abound in healthy grasslands.
20. These insects thrive in the African savannas where they build large mound nests.

Antarctica	**carbon**	**herbivore**	**rhizomes**	**tornadoes**
birds	**cheetahs**	**invertebrates**	**seed dispersal**	**tortoise**
burrow	**feathers**	**predators**	**sunflower**	**trees**
camouflage	**grass**	**reptile**	**termites**	**wildfire**

5

WETLANDS

Discover!

DISCOVER!

Wetlands are wet areas of land where water saturates the ground for at least part of the year. Found in both coastal and inland regions, wetlands remove sediment from water, they filter pollutants from the water, and they absorb water and help control flooding in areas around them. Wetlands also provide homes for different animal species. Some populations of waterfowl use wetlands as a stopover during their long migrations. Populations of amphibians like frogs and salamanders may use wetlands as a nursery where they lay their eggs, and their tadpoles grow and develop. Wetlands are often classified in one of three groups: swamps, marshes, and bogs. While wetlands are a biome in themselves, sometimes they can be found in other biomes such as forests and grasslands.

Swamps can be found both near the coast and farther inland. These wetland forests have trees that are well adapted to water. Alligators, crayfish, and birds are examples of some of the animal species found in swampy regions. Marshes are another type of wetland, characterized by grasses and sedges as the dominant plant species. Often freshwater marshes have fertile soil deposited in them when rivers flood the areas around them. Saltwater marshes are grassy wetlands near the coast where the tide brings in salty sea water. Bogs are a type of wetland found in colder climates. Oxygen levels are low in bogs, and they are typically acidic. Bogs fill with water mainly by precipitation such as rain and snow.

Words from the Wild

Ecological succession: the process of an ecosystem's living and nonliving factors changing over time

Migration: movement of animals from one place to another in search of resources such as food, shelter, or potential mates

Salinity: amount of dissolved salts in a body of water

Brackish: water that is saltier than freshwater but less salty than ocean water; usually found where rivers meet the ocean

Water cycle: process by which water circles through Earth's atmosphere, land, and bodies of water

Groundwater: water in saturated areas of soil and rocks underground

Water table: boundary at the top of the saturated groundwater zone

085 WHAT MAKES A WETLAND?

What makes up a typical wetland? Color and review the diagram below that illustrates wetland succession, then answer the questions.

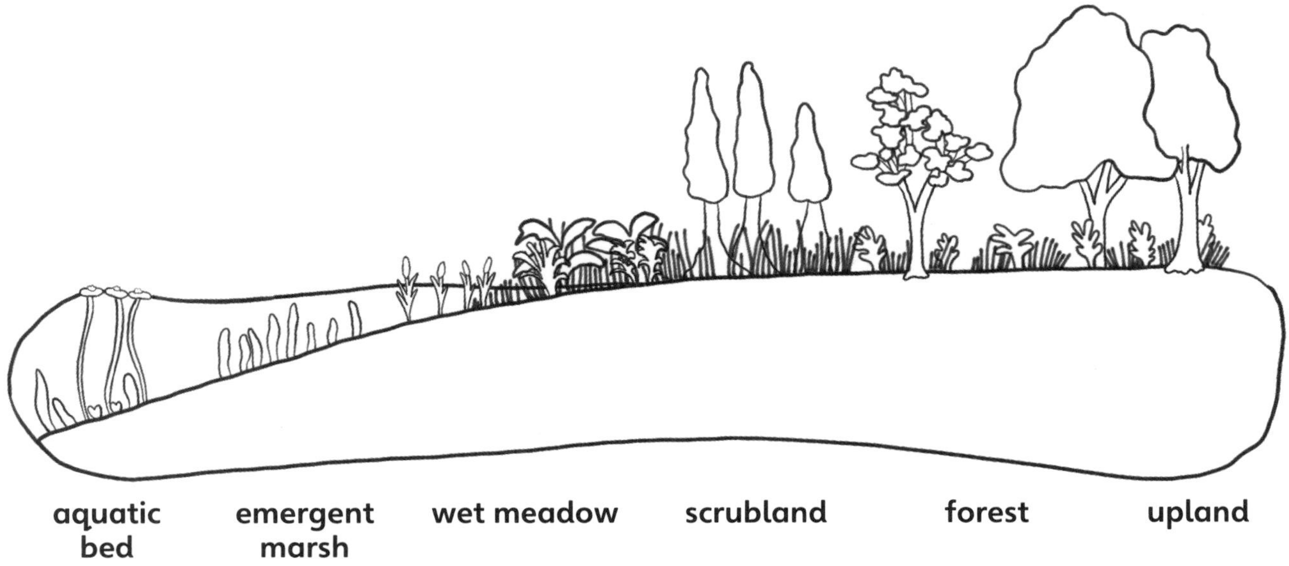

What do you observe about the plants as you travel upland from the water?

Ecological succession is the process of gradual changes that make up an ecosystem over time, usually after a disturbance of some kind. What disturbances might take place to create a wetland such as a swamp or marsh?

What are some other factors that might influence the composition of a wetland?

086 HOW MANY TYPES OF WETLANDS ARE THERE?

Wetlands can be divided into three main types: swamps, marshes, and bogs. Each are variations of wetlands with their own characteristic plants, animals, and soil. Color and match the illustrations below with the correct description.

swamp

colder climates, low oxygen levels, mosses, acidic soil

marsh

near the coast or inland, lots of trees, home to animals like alligators and crayfish

bog

saltwater or freshwater, can form when rivers flood, full of grasses

Did You Know? Coastal marshes protect the coast from large waves and erosion, and they provide habitat for animal species such as saltwater crocodiles in Australia as well as flamingos in the salt marshes of southern France.

087 HOW DO COASTAL WETLANDS WORK?

One of the important functions of coastal wetlands is the protection of the seashore and nearby areas along the coast. These wetlands prevent flooding and erosion along the coasts during storms like hurricanes. Hurricanes form over water when warm, moist air is pulled in from thunderstorms. The warm air converts into energy that begins **rotation**. The center of the storm forms an **eye** and **eyewall** as the ocean **water feeds the storm**. Within the eye, the pressure drops and **bands** of wind and rain that are **higher pressure** spread out from the center. The **Coriolis effect** due to Earth's rotation causes the storm to spin and dump huge amounts of water that cause flooding from the bands located in the **right front quadrant**. The hurricane grows and moves direction as **winds push the storm**.

Color the hurricane illustration and number the labels with the corresponding number from the diagram.

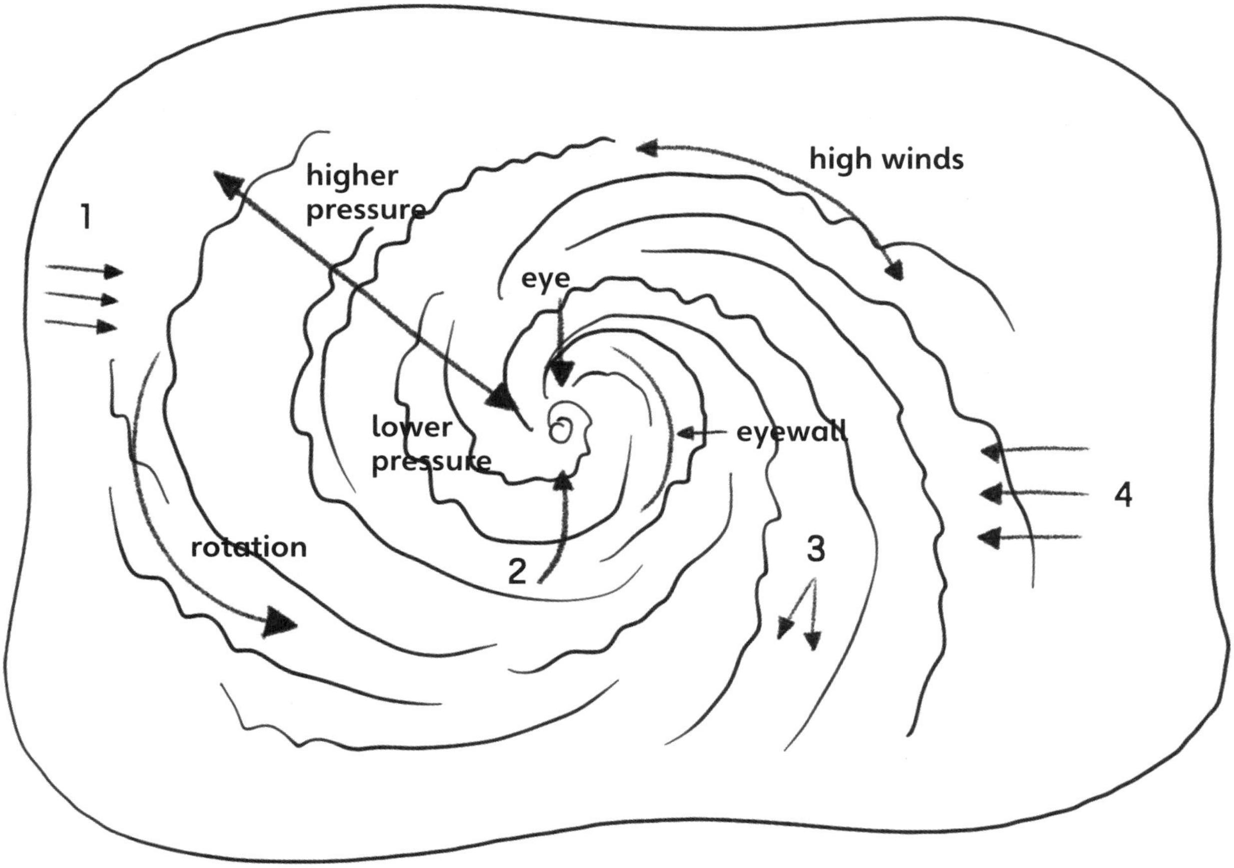

_____ water feeds storm

_____ Coriolis effect (spiral) air moves up through center of eye on outward

_____ bands

_____ winds push storm

088 HOW DO UNDERGROUND AQUIFERS WORK?

Fill in the blanks using the words below to learn more about underground aquifers.

confined	**recharging**	**water**
discharge	**underground**	

Aquifers are areas of porous rock or sediment ____________________ that store water. Wetlands can form from aquifers underground as they ____________________ to the surface. The larger the spaces between the rocks or sediment, the faster the water will flow. Aquifers may be ____________________ if they are covered with dense rock. Unconfined aquifers have softer soils above them. When it rains, ____________________ slowly seeps into these spaces and fills them up. This is called ____________________. Aquifers discharge naturally through places where they are exposed on Earth's surface such as springs and wetland areas.

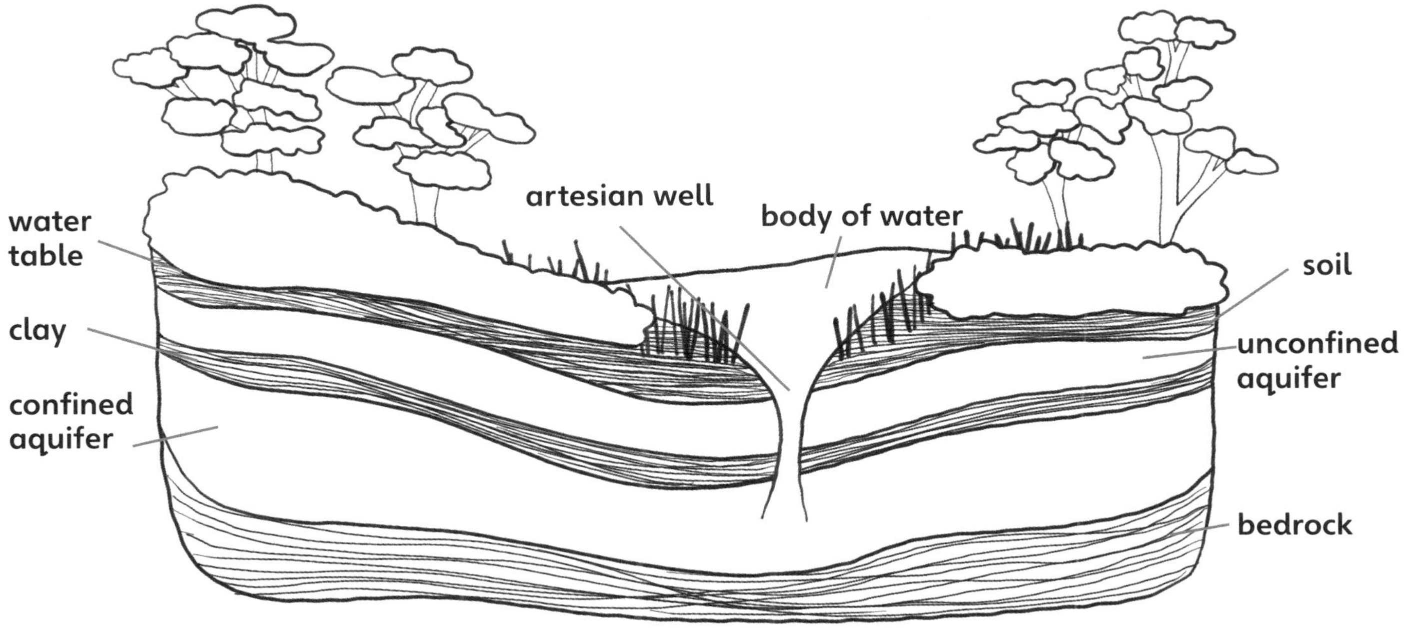

Did You Know? You have probably walked on water without even knowing it—groundwater, that is!

089 WHAT'S IN THE WATER?

One tiny drop from a wetland houses a world of microorganisms. These are living things too small to see with the naked eye.

Let's Explore! Collect some water from your local wetland, pond, creek, or puddle in your backyard. Take a look at a drop or two of the water using your microscope. You might be surprised to see that your drop of water is teeming with life.

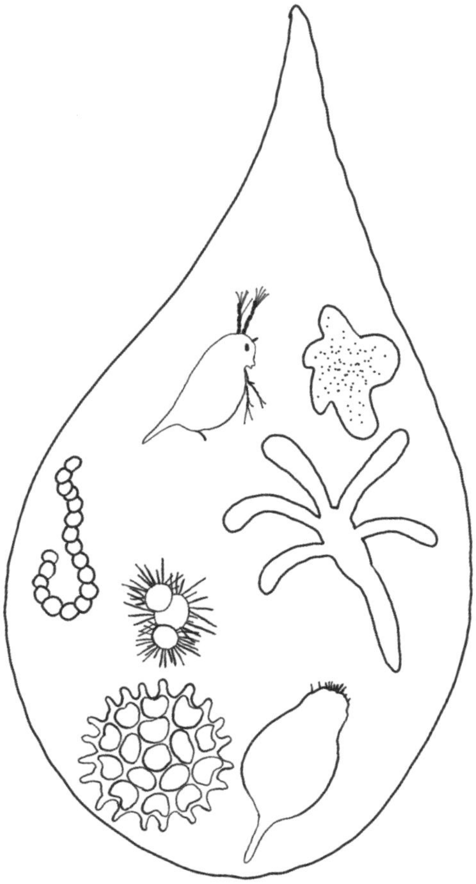

090 WHAT HAPPENS WHERE THE WATER MEETS THE SEA?

Unique ecosystems form where rivers merge and empty into oceans. The water in these areas is neither perfectly fresh nor super salty—it's brackish.

Color the illustration below using three different colors to represent water with three levels of salinity: **seawater** (ocean), **brackish water** (sea and freshwater mix), and **freshwater** (rivers and lakes).

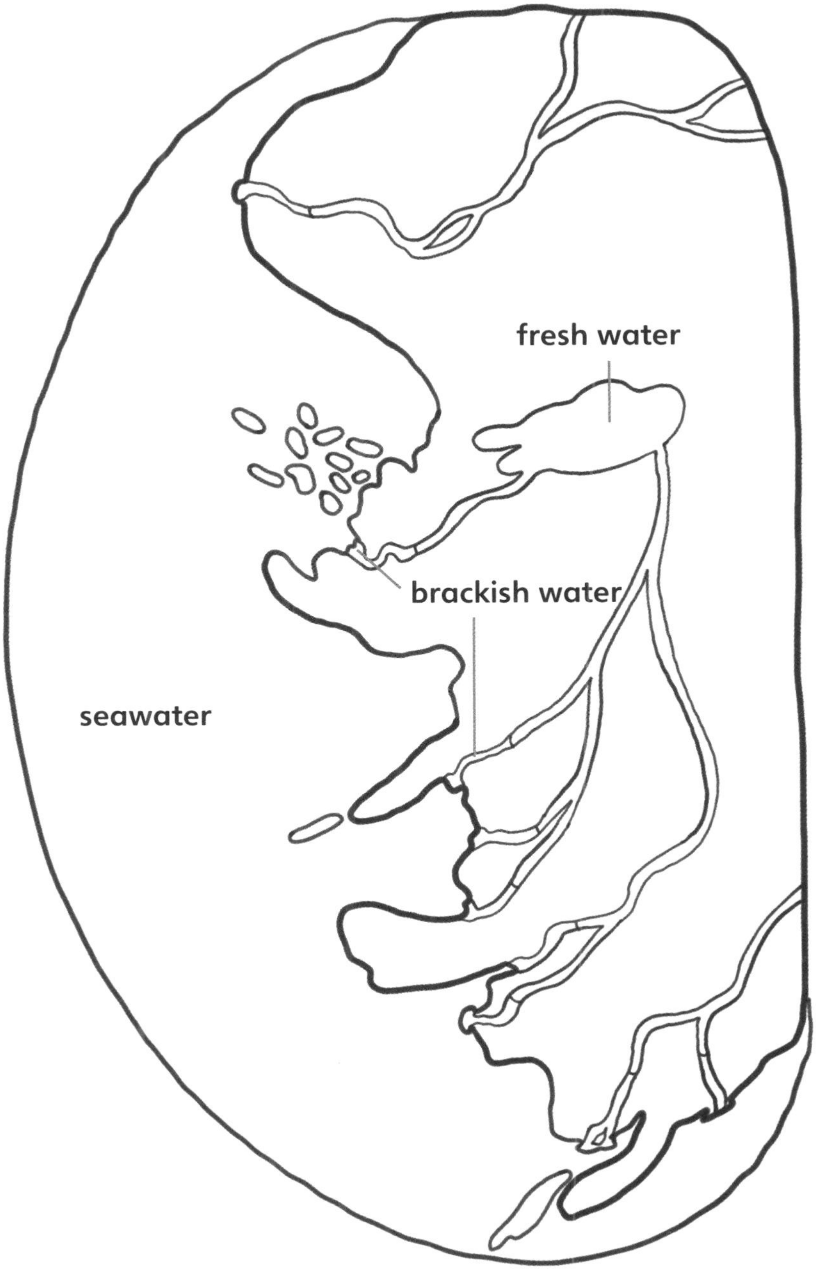

Let's Explore! Get a large glass jar, salt, water, and a golf ball. Fill the jar with approximately 1¼ cups (300 ml) of water. Then, put the golf ball in the water. Does the golf ball sink or float? Next, take the golf ball out, and add about 1/16 teaspoon (70 mg) of salt to the water and stir until the salt is dissolved. Put the golf ball back in the water. What happens to the golf ball? What can you conclude about the ability of objects to float in freshwater versus saltwater?

091 HOW DOES THE WATER CYCLE WORK?

Water flows through the Earth and floats through the atmosphere in an ongoing process called the water cycle. The water in your glass today may have been in a wetland at one point!

In the chart below, match each stage of the water cycle in the diagram with the descriptions provided by writing the name of the stage in the left column.

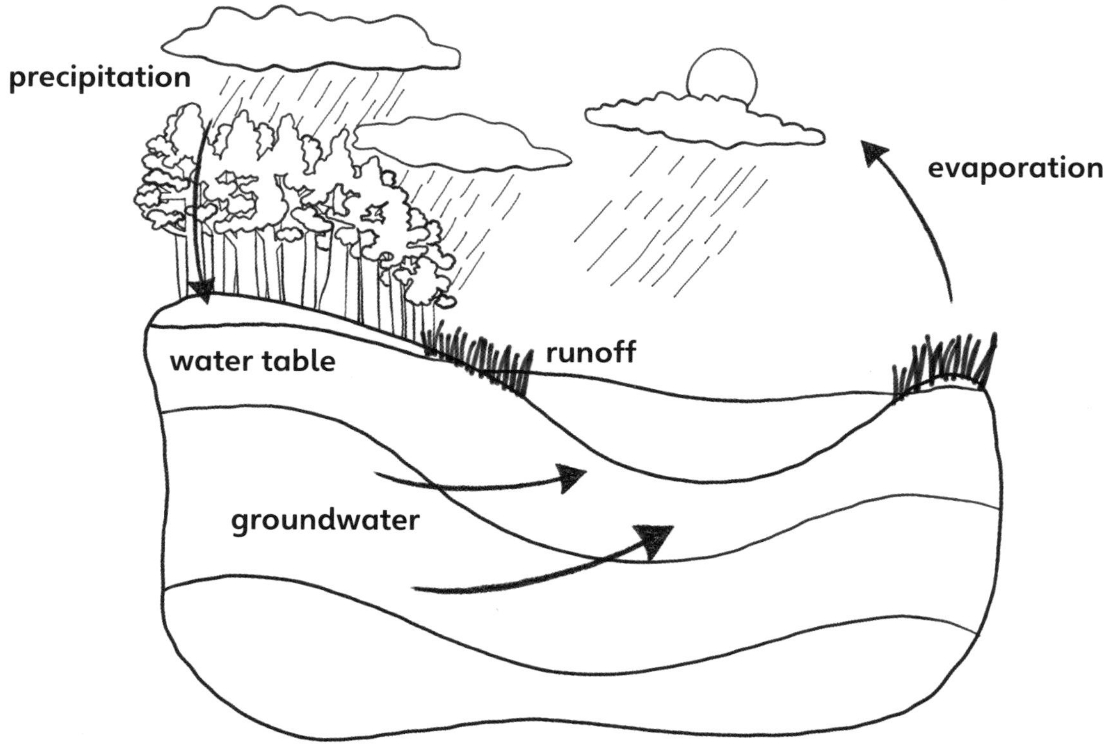

	The Sun heats up water on the Earth's surface, causing its molecules to move around so quickly, they become a gas that rises up into the atmosphere.
	When it cools off in the sky, it condenses into clouds, and if enough water gathers together, this falls to the ground.
	As rain falls to the Earth, it may soak into the ground, creating levels of saturation.
	This water can recharge aquifers underground and raise the water table.
	If the ground is saturated and cannot soak up the water, or if the water hits roadways or other hard surfaces, it will eventually catch up with a body of water like a stream, wetland, or ocean.

092 CAN YOU IDENTIFY THE DIFFERENT TYPES OF ALGAE?

While algae are able to use sunlight and carbon dioxide to make their own food like plants do, they are actually protists! Protists do not belong to the animal, plant, or fungi kingdoms. They have a classification of their own, the kingdom Protista.

In wetlands, algae create oxygen for the ecosystem and provide food for a variety of creatures living there, such as fish and invertebrates. They also provide shelter for invertebrates and help keep them from drying out when the wetland water level is low.

Label the diagram below based on the location descriptions given for each alga.

metaphyton (on surface) | **epiphyton** (on plants) | **epidendron** (on dead wood) | **epipelon** (on sediments) | **epilithon** (on rocks)

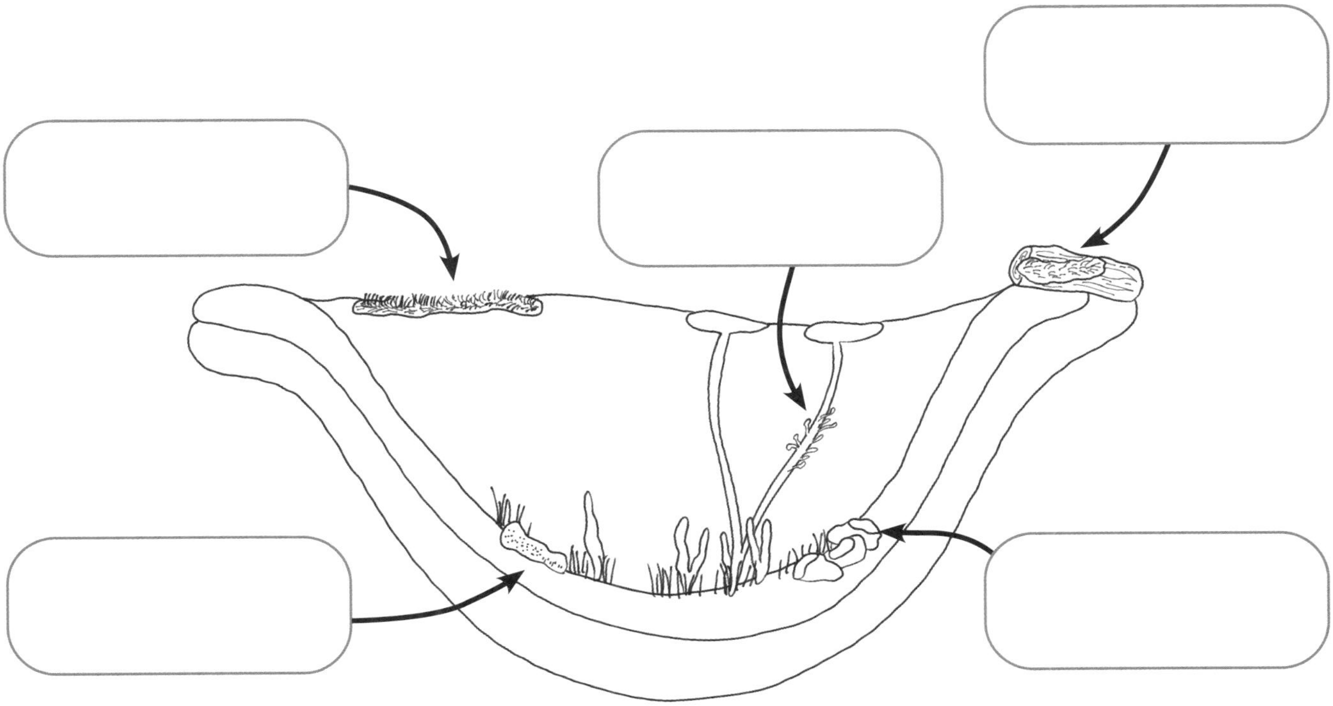

Let's Explore! Visit a local wetland or other body of water and look for algae on top of the water or on rocks, wood, or plants underneath the water's surface.

093 WHAT DO YOU KNOW ABOUT WETLAND PLANTS?

The different types of wetlands are often categorized by the plants that grow in them. Mosses grow across bog surfaces, grasses grow in marshes, and trees grow up out of swamps. Wetland plants are influenced by water type (fresh or salty) as well as how long the wetland has water in it during the year.

Can you match each wetland plant-themed vocabulary term with the correct definition?

aerial roots	an organic soil that forms in bogs from layers of slowly decaying plant material over many years
emergent plants	completely underwater or submerged in the wetland
floating plants	plants with leaves and flowers that sit on the wetland's surface
moss	roots anchor them in the soil while their leaves and stems "emerge" from the water
peat	roots growing above the ground
submerged plants	spongy and soft, these small plants grow together to create a carpet

094 WHO LIVES IN THE WETLANDS?

Swamps, marshes, and bogs are home to a variety of animals. Wetlands have food, water, and shelter, making them a perfect habitat for many creatures.

Use the hints to help you identify the different types of wetland animals.

Hint: Large mammals that live in sub-Saharan African wetlands.

____

Hint: Rodents native to North America and are well-adapted to living in wetlands.

____

Hint: Will often jump into the water to hide when startled by a predator.

____

Hint: The largest species in the deer family—and can swim!

____

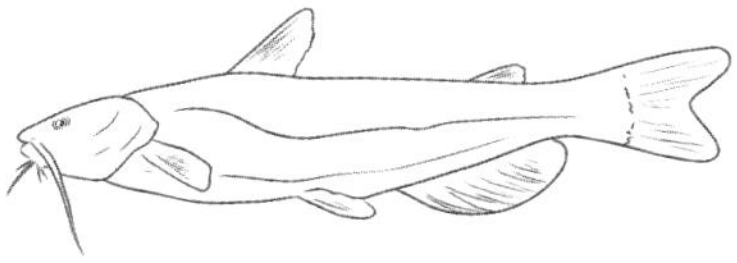

Hint: These fish get their name from their distinctive barbels, which resemble a cat's whiskers.

____

Let's Explore! Look for traces of animal activity the next time you visit a wetland area. Check for footprints, scat, nests, holes, or leftovers from a meal. Muddy edges of wetlands are the perfect place to find footprints and food scraps.

095 WHAT DO YOU KNOW ABOUT THE AWESOME OPOSSUM?

Fill in the blanks using the words below to learn more about the only marsupial in most of North America who makes wetlands their home.

marsupials	**nocturnal**	**omnivores**	**pouch**	**prehensile**

Opossums are ________________, so wetlands provide both plant and animal food for their diet. They eat a variety of insects, small animals, seeds, and fruits. They are a ________________ creature, climbing trees and swimming when needed to find a meal. Their ________________ tails and opposable thumbs help them in the trees. Opossums are ________________, and they carry and nurse their young in a pouch until the babies are fully developed. Once they're able to leave the ________________, young "joeys" may hitch a ride on their mother's back to move from place to place.

096 WHO EATS WHAT IN THE WETLANDS?

With many insects, fish, and amphibians, wetlands around the world are attractive to predators. Predators in marshes, swamps, and bogs range in size, from tiny invertebrates like beetles to huge hunters like saltwater crocodiles.

Create your own wetland food chain by drawing your favorite wetland predator along with its prey. Don't forget to include what the prey animal eats and so on. Describe each link in the chain.

Let's Explore! Visit a wetland ecosystem to see if you can find a wetland food chain in action. Maybe you'll find a bird catching a dragonfly or evidence of a raccoon hunting for crayfish.

097 WHAT'S THE DIFFERENCE?

Alligators and crocodiles are both reptiles in the order Crocodylia. They are covered in protective scales and are cold-blooded predators. Crocodiles can grow larger than alligators, and crocodiles have longer, pointier snouts. An alligator usually has darker gray coloring while crocodiles are a lighter greenish-brown color. And alligators' lower teeth are not visible when their mouth is closed. Most alligators prefer freshwater habitats while crocodiles are found in both freshwater and saltwater.

Complete the Venn diagram to compare and contrast alligators and crocodiles. One circle should contain the characteristics of alligators while the other should highlight the characteristics of crocodiles. The overlapping space in the middle should include features shared by both.

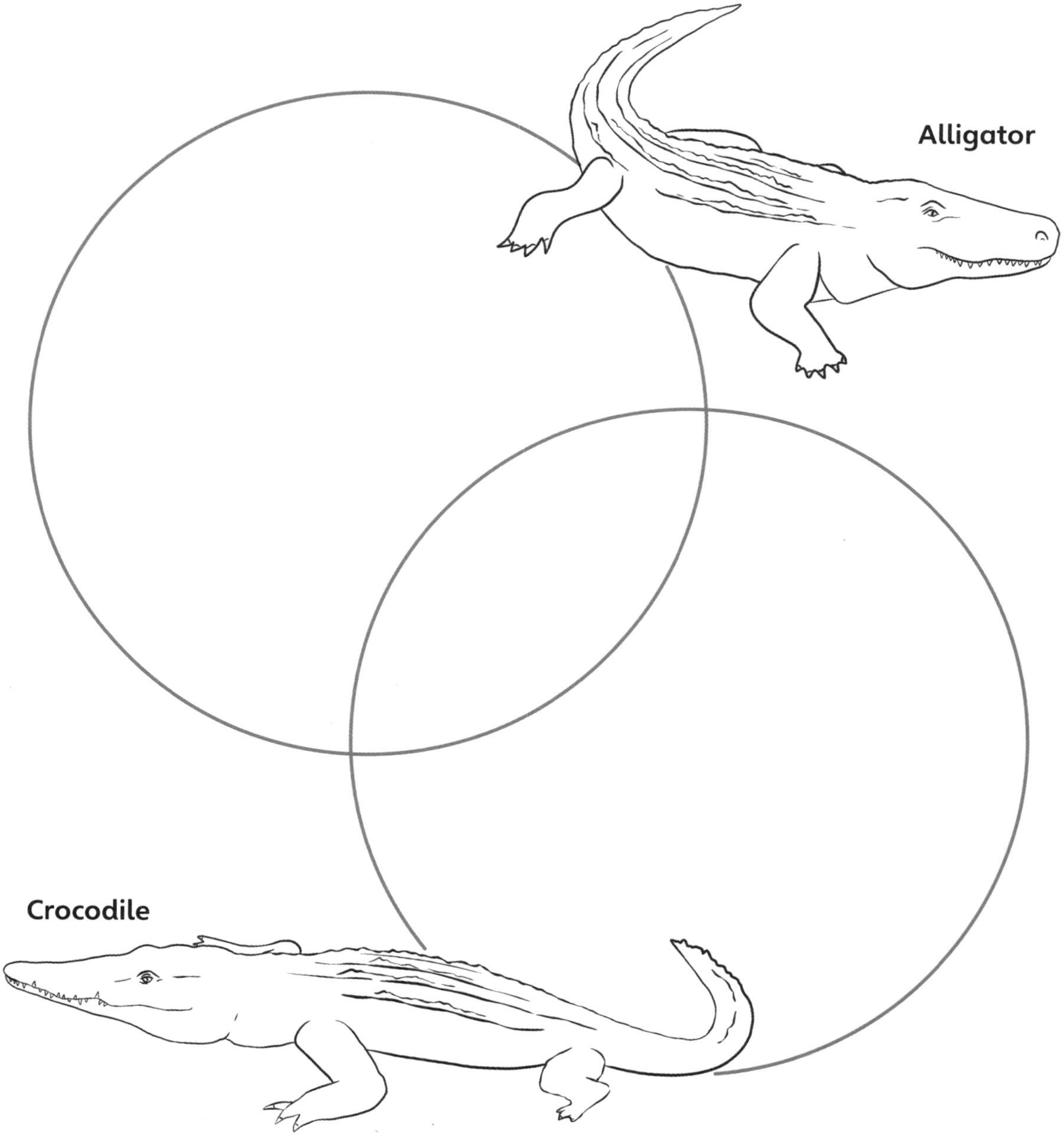

098 WHY DO BIRDS NEED WETLANDS?

Fill in the blanks using the words below to learn more about birds in wetlands.

camouflaged **migration** **nest** **stopover** **water**

Wetlands provide important habitats for birds. They ______________ in wetlands, using abundant vegetation as shelter and cover to hide their eggs and young. Their feather patterns help birds stay ______________. Birds like waterfowl find wetlands along their ______________ routes to use as ______________ points where they can eat and rest before moving on. Birds find food in wetland ecosystems. They may eat plants, fish, insects, and small animals in wetlands. They look for food in the soil, take vegetation or prey from the water, grab small animals from the surrounding land, or even find tiny creatures on plants in the ______________.

Let's Explore! Find an open area or high ground where you have a good view of the sky, and look for migrating birds. You can check migration forecasts to see when birds might be on the move. You can also look for pairs of waterfowl, like geese and ducks, that have nested near wetlands or have their babies with them.

099 WHY ARE SOME WETLAND WATERFOWL SO COLORFUL?

Sexual dimorphism refers to the differences in features exhibited by males and females of a species—in this case, wetland waterfowl. Males often have brighter colors or special feathers to attract females while the females are patterned to blend in with their surroundings as they sit on the nest.

Color this pair of wood ducks to show the dimorphism between the male and female of the species.

100 HOW ARE TURTLES ADAPTED TO WETLANDS?

Aquatic turtles like the common snapping turtle can often be found in freshwater or brackish habitats that have still water, like ponds and wetlands. Their heads are large, and their jaws are powerful. They “snap” to grab prey and also as a defense mechanism. Common snapping turtles eat a variety of animals like fish, birds, mammals, and amphibians. They may also eat carrion and plants.

Color and label the snapping turtle using the words below.

clawed toes **ridged carapace (upper shell)** **sharp beak**

long tail **strong jaw**

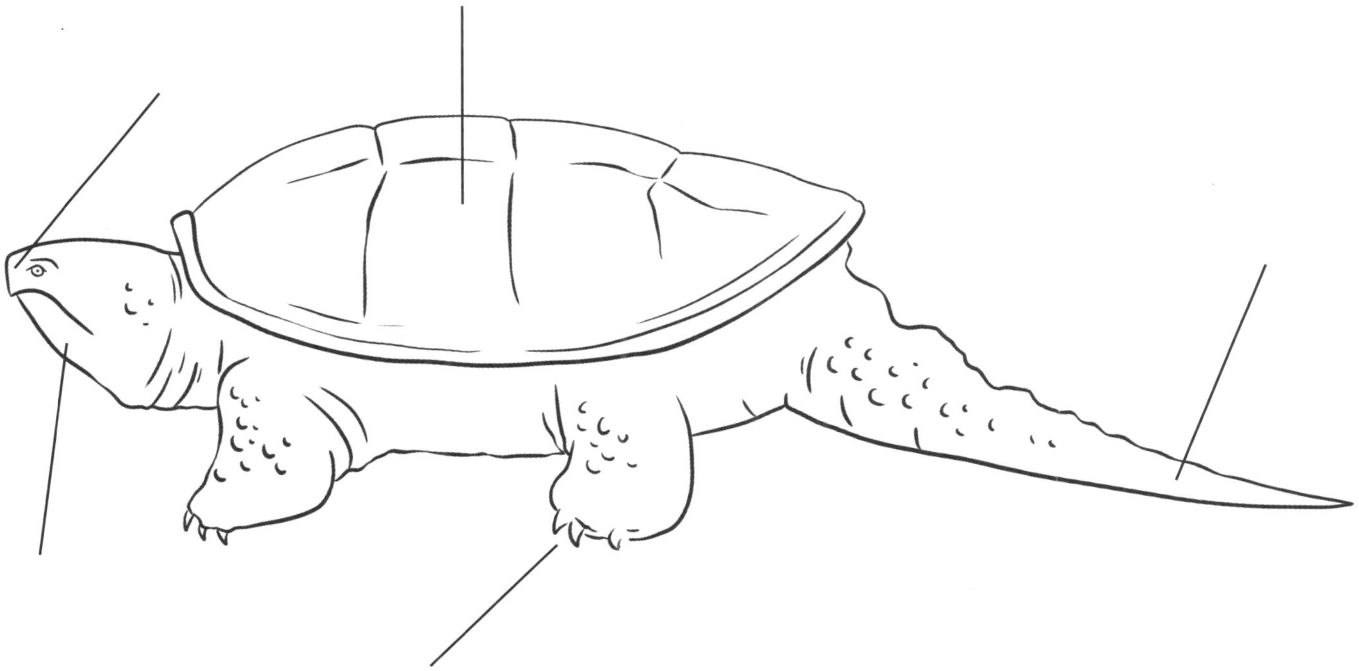

Let's Explore! Visit a wetland near you! If you don't live near a wetland, choose another aquatic habitat to visit instead. Keep an eye out for a reptile or amphibian species you can record in your nature journal.

101 WHY IS ECDYSIS IMPORTANT?

Read the information about ecdysis, then decide if the statements below are true or false.

When reptiles grow, they must shed their outer layer of scales in a process called ecdysis. Shedding not only allows reptiles to grow, but it also helps them repair skin injuries and get rid of parasites they may be carrying on their outer layer. Amphibians also shed their skin, often eating it afterward, possibly for a source of nutrients. Scientists believe ecdysis in amphibians may help keep their skin soft and free from bacteria and fungi.

T or F Shedding their skin allows reptiles to grow.

T or F Reptiles may eat the skin they shed for extra nutrients.

T or F The shedding process usually starts at the tail end.

T or F Reptiles are the only animals that shed their skin.

T or F Shedding helps animals to get rid of parasites or microbes they have on their skin.

102 MOSQUITOES: IRRITATING OR IMPORTANT?

Both larvae and adults provide food for many wetland creatures. Over 3,000 species of mosquitoes buzz around the planet, most commonly near aquatic habitats.

Read the facts about the mosquito life cycle. Color and label each by writing the correct number next to each stage.

1. eggs **2. larva** **3. pupa** **4. adult**

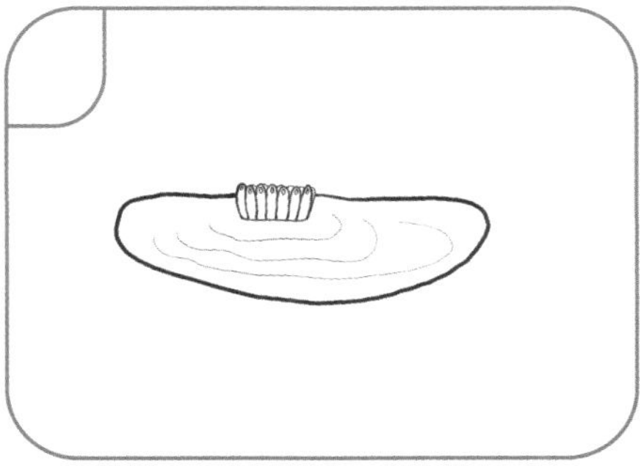

Females drink blood to get the protein they need for making eggs.

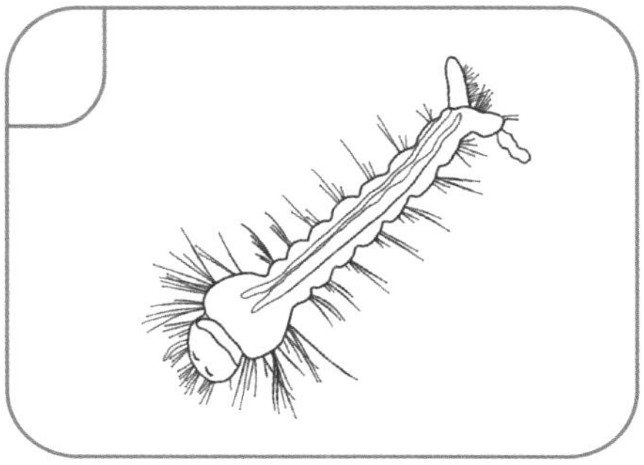

Larvae hatch from eggs in standing water, where they feed on bacteria and organic matter.

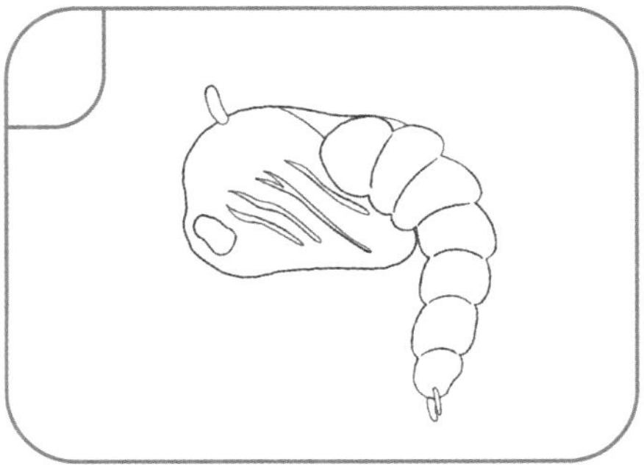

Their pupal stage takes up to two weeks to form.

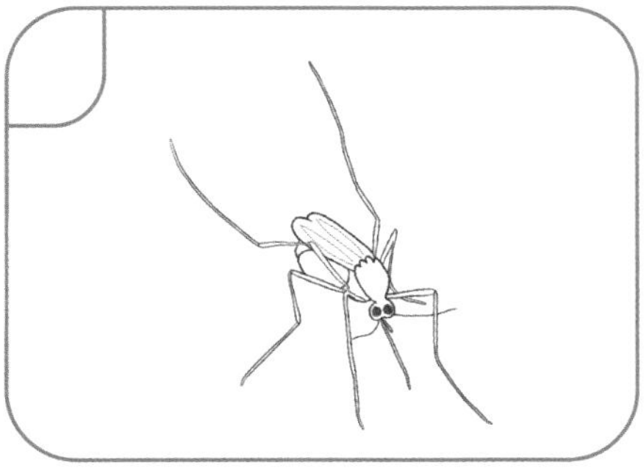

When the adult emerges, it must rest and dry out before taking flight.

Let's Explore! Next time you visit a wetland, closely examine the water. Did you see any invertebrates in the water? Maybe a mosquito larva or another aquatic insect?

103 HOW DO DRAGONFLIES DOMINATE THE WETLAND ECOSYSTEM?

Dragonfly nymphs start their lives in wetland habitats about a week after the female dragonfly lays her eggs. They grow slowly, taking several months to mature into adults. While developing, dragonflies feed on insect eggs and larvae, including other nymphs, in their aquatic home.

Complete the dragonfly symmetry activity by drawing the blank half of the dragonfly to match the other.

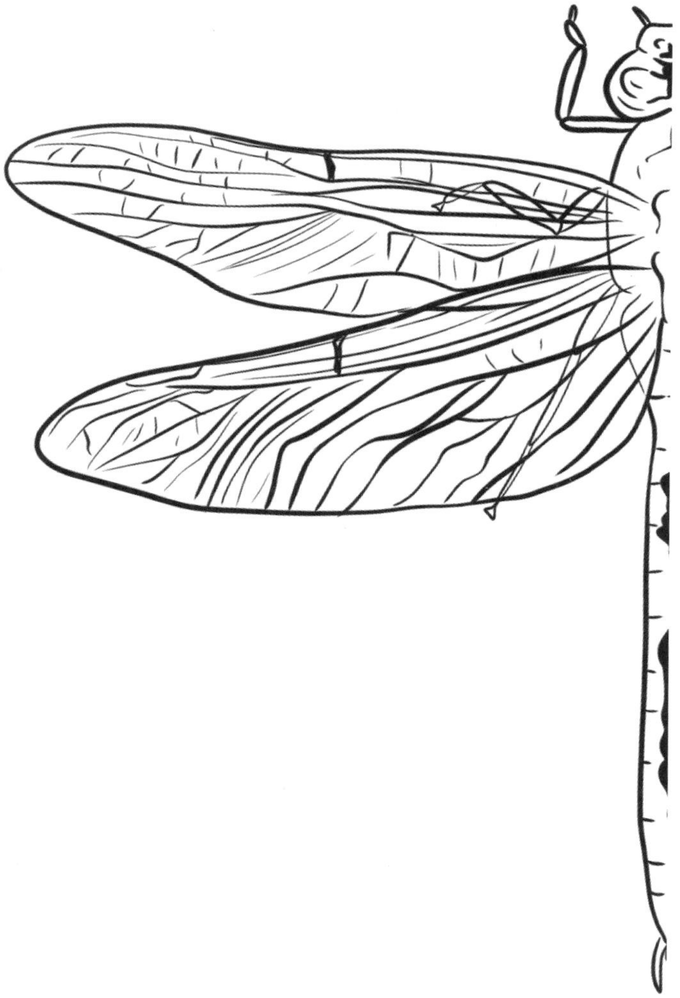

104 WHAT'S IN A WETLAND?

Visit a wetland area, whether saltwater or freshwater. Observe the vast array of living things, from tiny insects to large wading birds. Maybe there are even mammals visiting the wetland for a drink of water or to make their home along the shore. Notice the plants by the water's edge and the plants in the water itself. What species of trees grow there? Jot down what you see in the wetland, and sketch a picture of the ecosystem.

105 WETLAND QUIZ

Test your knowledge by answering these questions using the word bank below.

1. What is the process of gradual changes that make up an ecosystem over time? ____________
2. These wetlands can form when rivers flood and are full of grasses. ____________
3. This type of wetland has low oxygen levels, mosses, and acidic soil. ____________
4. Which wetland is near the coast or inland and has lots of trees and animals like alligators and crayfish? ____________
5. This describes the differences in features between males and females in a species. ____________
6. These are areas of porous rock found underground. ____________
7. Coastal wetlands protect the coasts from storms like these. ____________
8. One tiny drop of wetland water is full of these. ____________
9. What type of water forms when seawater meets freshwater? ____________
10. What is the ongoing process by which water flows through the Earth and floats through the atmosphere? ____________
11. While many people think of these as plants, they are actually protists. ____________
12. Some wetland trees have these types of roots that grow above ground. ____________
13. What type of soil forms over many years in bogs from layers of slowly decaying plant material? ____________
14. What is the largest species in the deer family and may be found swimming in wetlands? ____________
15. These rough-scaled reptiles prey on animals that live in or near the water. ____________
16. Birds often use wetlands as stopover points during this long journey. ____________
17. What reptiles have hard shells, large heads, and powerful jaws? ____________
18. What is the process called when reptiles and amphibians shed their outer layer of scales as they grow? ____________
19. Females of this family of insects drink blood to get the protein they need for making eggs. ____________
20. These flying insects feed on prey like mosquitoes. ____________

aerial roots	**crocodilians**	**marsh**	**peat**
algae	**dimorphism**	**microorganisms**	**snapping turtles**
aquifers	**dragonfly**	**migration**	**succession**
bog	**ecdysis**	**moose**	**swamp**
brackish	**hurricanes**	**mosquitoes**	**the water cycle**

001

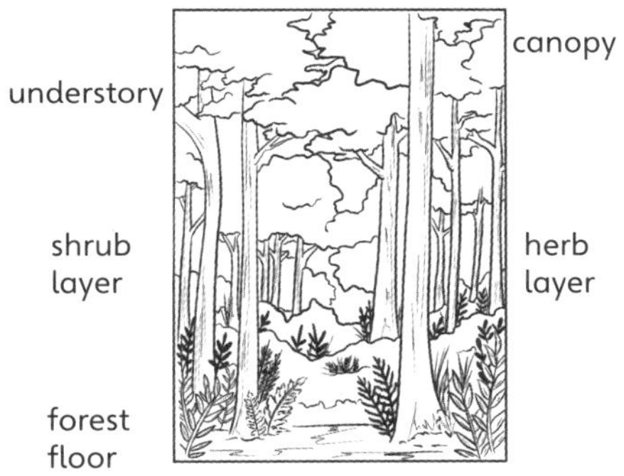

002

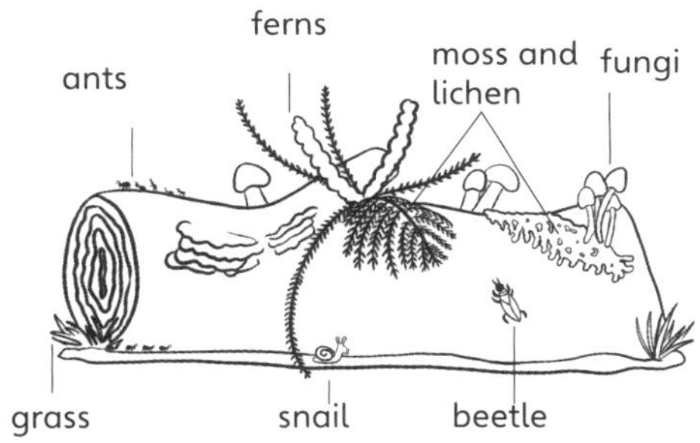

005

broadleaf
chlorophyll
deciduous
dormant
photosynthesis

a tree or plant with wide flat leaves
falling off or shedding seasonally
process used by plants to convert sunlight into energy
responsible for the green color of many plants
the suspension or slowing down of physical functions for a period of time

008

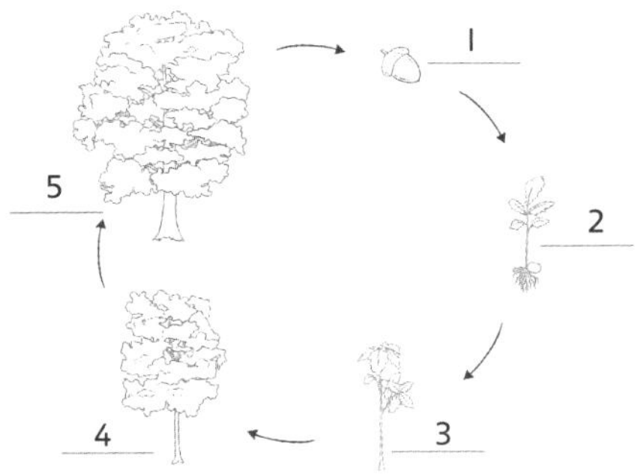

009

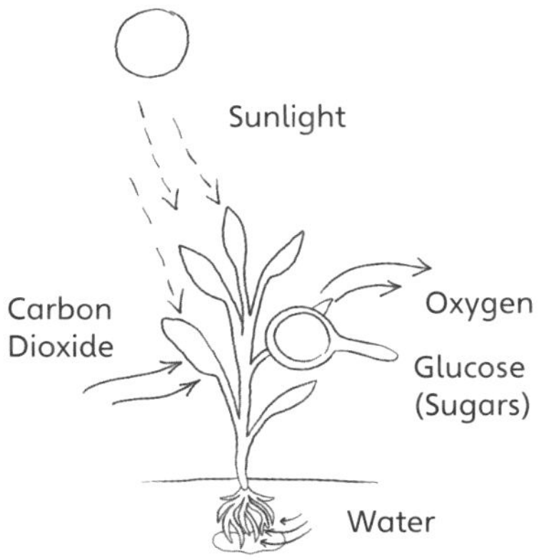

011

012

T
F
T
T
T
F

015

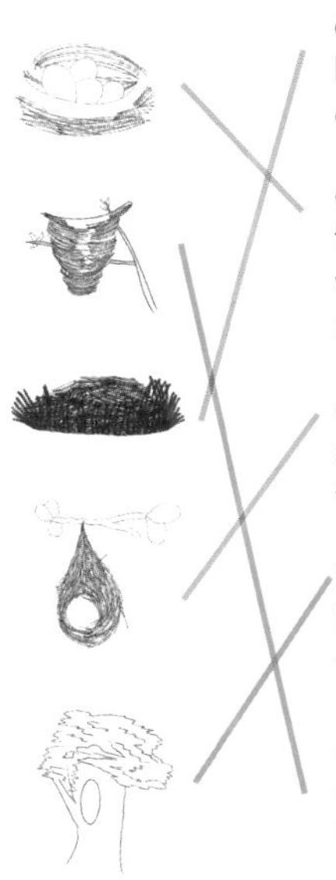

a pile of materials built in a depression on the ground

a shallow hole in the ground lined with sticks and other materials

an elongated pouch suspended from a tree branch

built in natural hollows such as trees cavities

cup-shaped with a deep rounded hollow in the center

016

017

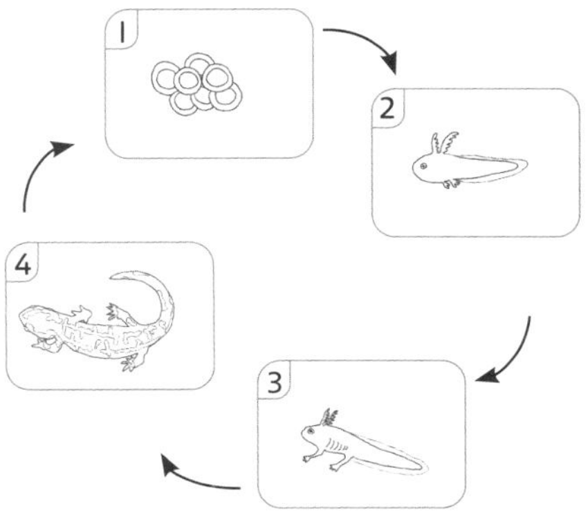

021

1. canopy 2. decomposers 3. abiotic 4. seasons 5. chlorophyll 6. transpiration 7. deciduous 8. bark 9. acorn 10. photosynthesis 11. fungi 12. tracks 13. hibernate 14. prey 15. omnivore 16. nests 17. tadpole 18. web 19. evergreen 20. scat

024

1. fluctuating temperatures
2. precipitation
3. wind
4. previous water source
5. water evaporation

026

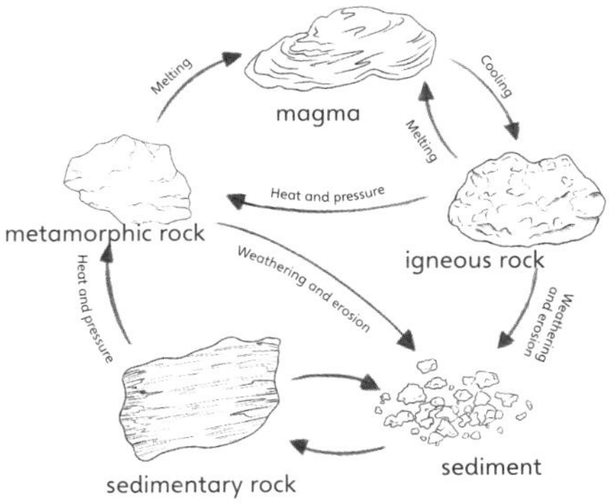

028

1. bats
2. butterflies
3. hummingbird
4. bees

029

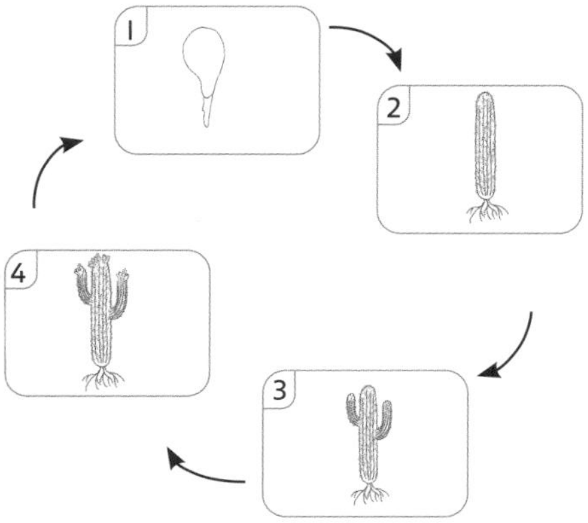

030

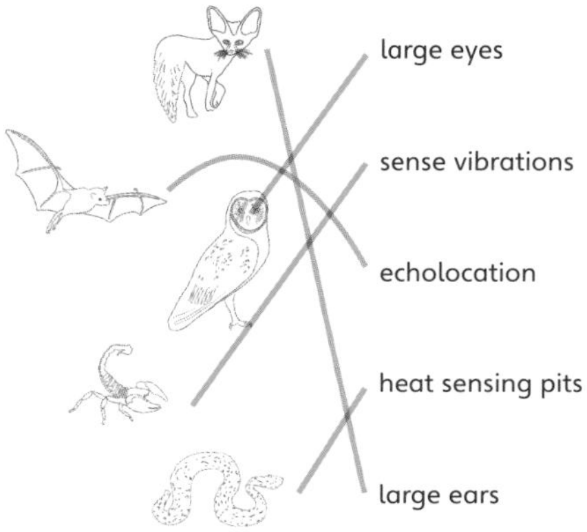

032

Amphibian: frog, salamander, toad

Bird: cactus, wren, golden eagle, ostrich peregrine falcon, roadrunner

Invertebrate: centipede, locust, scorpion, sphinx moth, tarantula

Mammal: big brown bat, camel, fennec fox, jackrabbit, javelina

Reptile: bearded dragon, Gila monster, goanna rattlesnake, tortoise

034

wolf

035

3 primary flight feathers
2 secondary flight feathers
1 coverts

037

1. temperature
2. dormant
3. energy
4. amphibians
5. underground

038

camouflage
cold-blooded
nocturnal
reptile
scales
venom

a small, rigid protective plate that grows out of an animal's skin

active at night and sleeps during the day

cold-blooded, air-breathing vertebrate with body covered in scales and/or scutes

defense tactic used to disguise appearance

having a body temperature that varies with the environment

highly toxic saliva containing toxins that immobilize prey

039

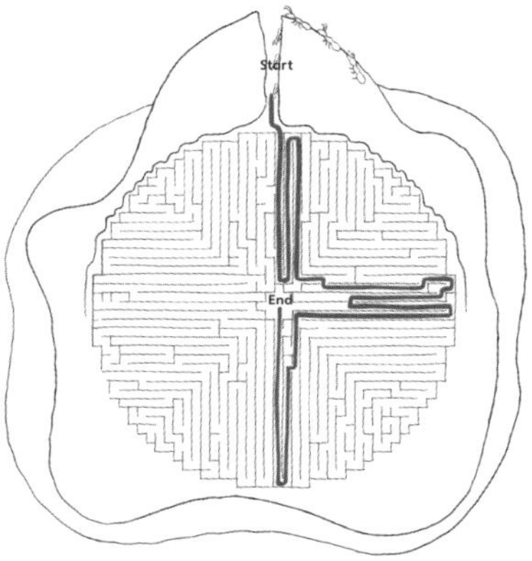

042

1. camouflage 2. raptor 3. migration
4. evaporation 5. aestivation 6. predator
7. landforms 8. nocturnal 9. xerocole
10. pollinator 11. erosion 12. cactus
13. sedimentary rock 14. igneous rock
15. adaptations 16. metamorphic rock
17. arid 18. colony 19. dormancy
20. burrows

043

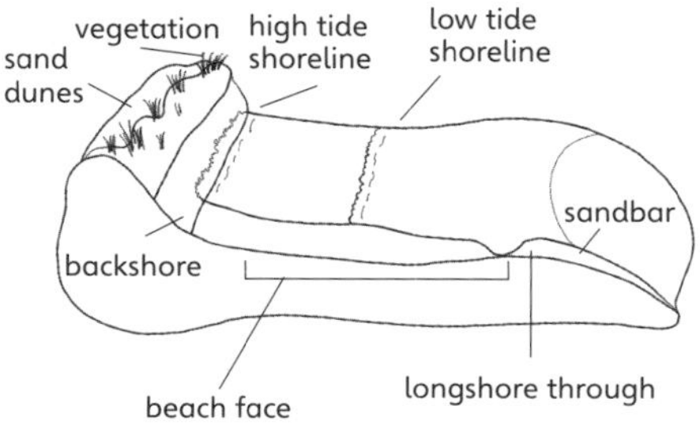

044

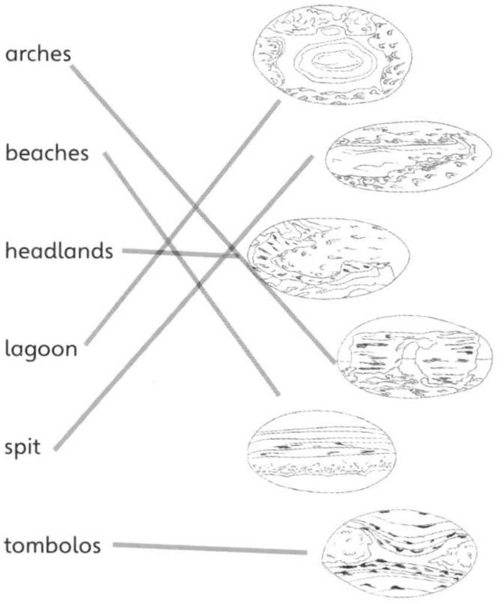

046

sand
coasts
flooding
adapted
shelter

047

epipelagic
mesopelagic
bathypelagic
abyssopelagic
hadalpelagic

048

biodiversity
coast
erosion
ocean
Pacific
sand
tide
wave

area of land next to the ocean

daily rise and fall of the ocean's water caused by the gravitational pull of the Moon and Sun

Earth's largest and deepest ocean

energy moving through the water, often caused by wind

formed from weathering of rocks and carried and deposited through the process of erosion

large expanse of salt water covering Earth

the carrying away of sediment

the variety of living things living in an area

049

beach
waves
tide
twice
Moon

050

052

exoskeleton
mollusks
gills
seashores

053

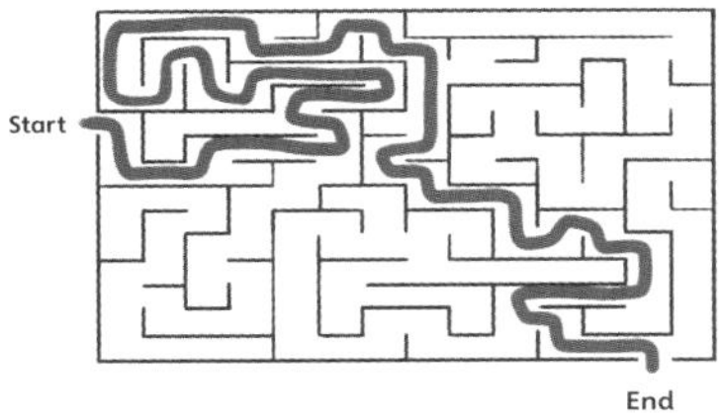

054

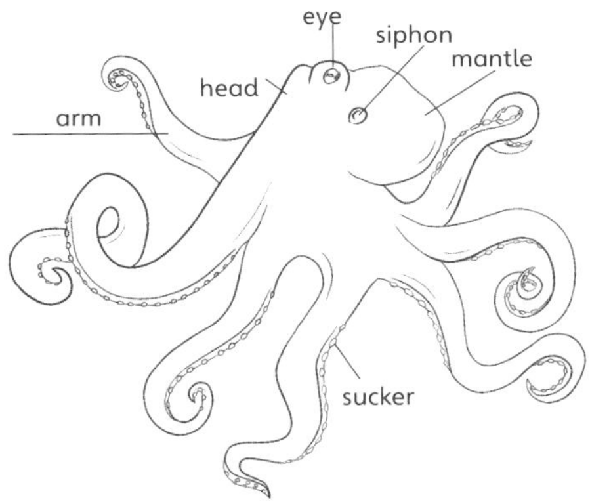

055

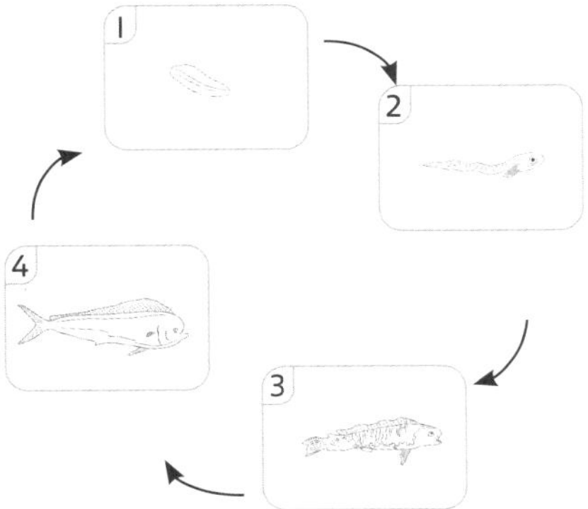

056

T
F
T
T
F

059

spouts
breached
fluke
dorsal fin

060

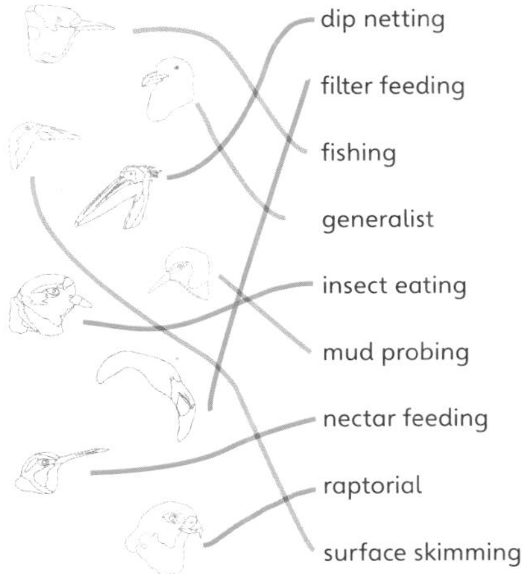

061

seashore
niches
adaptations
invertebrates

063

1. seashore 2. dunes 3. coastal landforms
4. sand 5. ocean zones 6. the ocean
7. waves 8. intertidal zone 9. tide
10. Moon 11. tide pool 12. seashells
13. sea turtles 14. octopuses 15. sharks
16. fish 17. marine mammals 18. dorsal fin
19. gull 20. beak

064

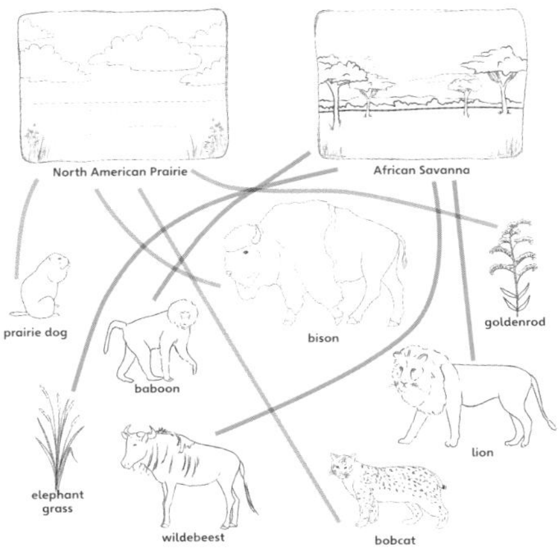

065

T
T
F
T
F

066

2
1
3
5
4

067

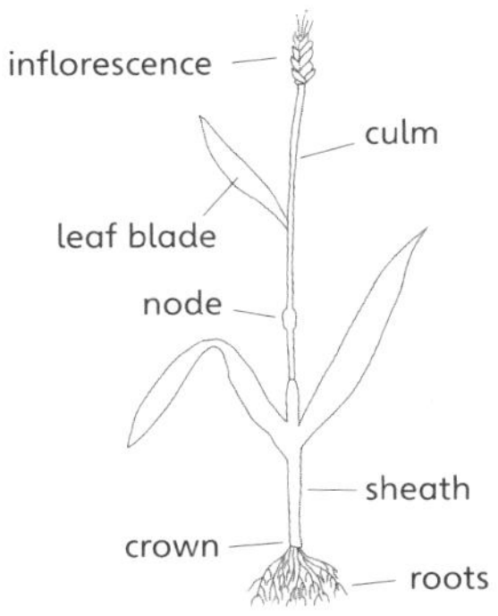

068

carbon dioxide, to use for photosynthesis, soil

069

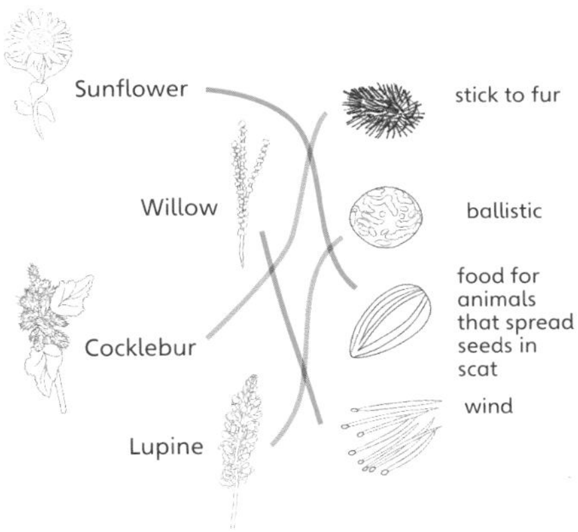

071

Carnivore: African wild dog, bobcat, cheetah, eagle, lion

Herbivore: bison, elephant, giraffe, kangaroo, pronghorn, wildebeest, zebra, prairie dog

Omnivore: tortoise, coyote, baboon

072

075

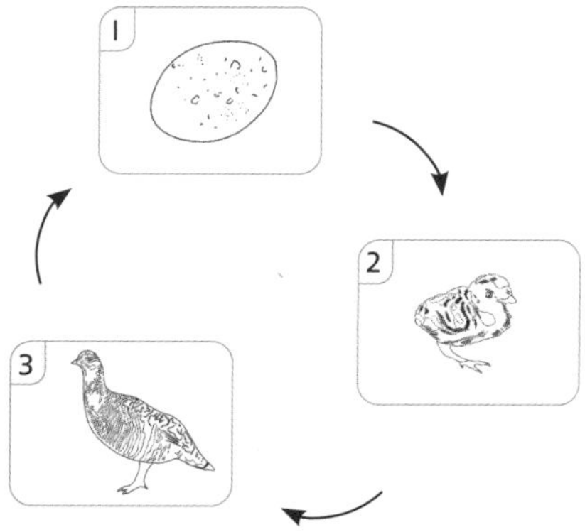

078

eggs
hatchlings
parents
crocodilians
predators

080

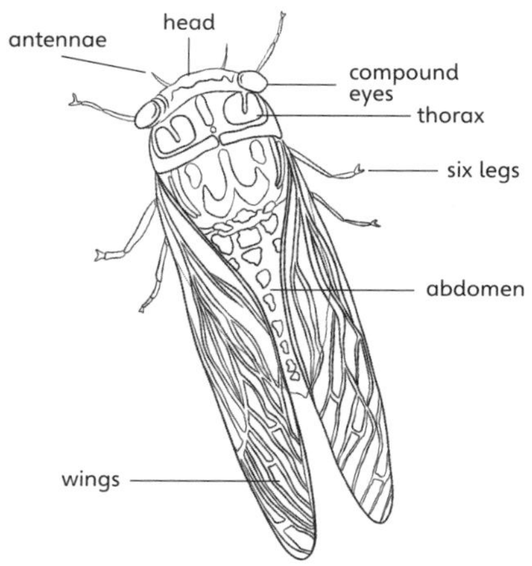

081

082

savannas
mound
aerate
rotting wood
pollinate

084

1. Antarctica 2. wildfire 3. tornadoes
4. grass 5. rhizomes 6. carbon
7. seed dispersal 8. sunflower 9. trees
10. herbivore 11. burrow 12. predators
13. cheetahs 14. camouflage 15. birds
16. feathers 17. reptile 18. tortoise
19. invertebrates 20. termites

086

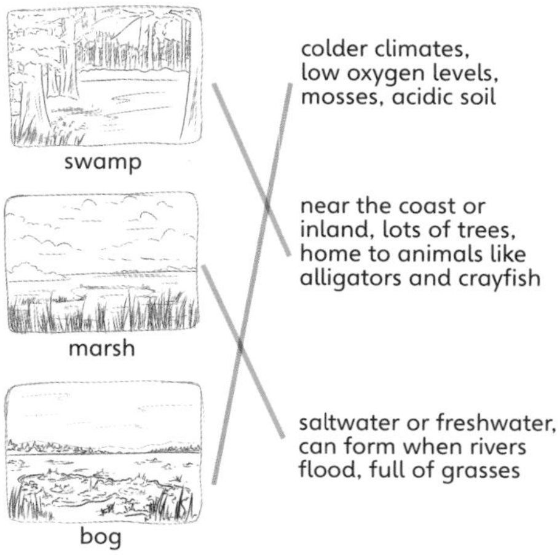

087

1
4
2
3

088

underground
discharge
confined
water
recharging

090

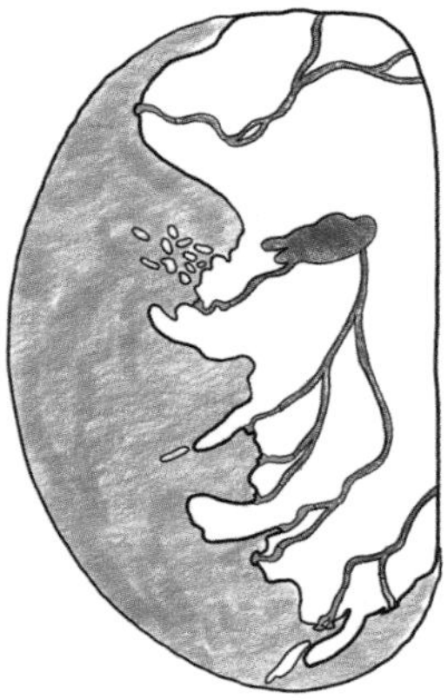

091

evaporation
precipitation
water table
groundwater
runoff

092

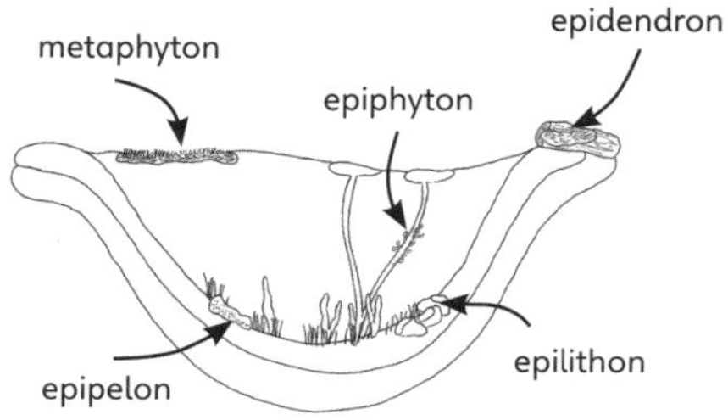

093

aerial roots
emergent plants
floating plants
moss
peat
submerged plants

an organic soil that forms in bogs from layers of slowly decaying plant material over many years
completely underwater or submerged in the wetland
plants with leaves and flowers that sit on the wetland's surface
roots anchor them in the soil while their leaves and stems "emerge" from the water
roots growing above the ground
spongy and soft, these small plants grow together to create a carpet

094

hippopotamus
muskrat
swamp rabbit
moose
catfish

095

omnivores
nocturnal
prehensile
marsupials
pouch

098

nest
camouflaged
migration
stopover
water

100

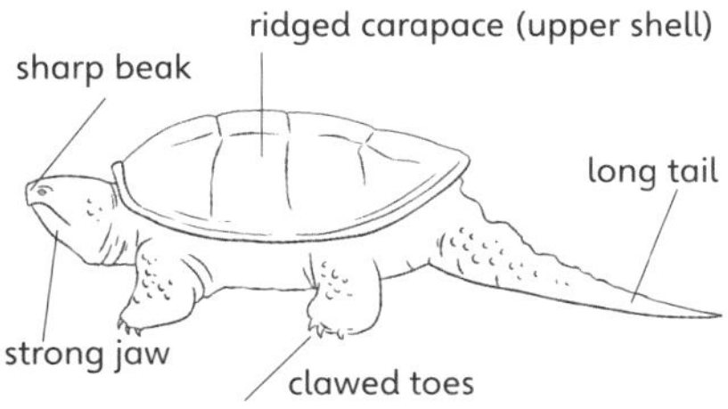

101

T
T
F
F
T

102

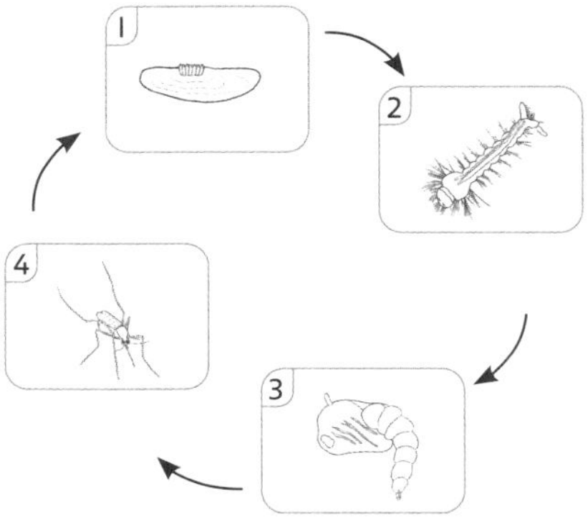

105

1. succession 2. marsh 3. bog 4. swamp 5. dimorphism 6. aquifers 7. hurricanes 8. microorganisms 9. brackish 10. water cycle 11. algae 12. aerial roots 13. peat 14. moose 15. crocodilians 16. migration 17. snapping turtles 18. ecdysis 19. mosquitoes 20. dragonfly

ACKNOWLEDGMENTS

LAUREN

A very special thank-you to my amazing husband for supporting me, my incredible children for inspiring me, and my parents for believing in me.

STEPHANIE

Special thanks to my husband and children for supporting and inspiring me every day. I also want to express my gratitude to my friends and coauthors, Laura and Lauren; I'm looking forward to many more years of creative collaboration with you both.

LAURA

I would like to thank my children for inspiring me to explore and study nature on a regular basis. And I would like to thank my husband for supporting my writing career and our children's education throughout this amazing process. Lastly, my heart is grateful to my parents for always encouraging my dreams, no matter what. We did it!

ABOUT THE AUTHORS

LAUREN GIORDANO is an author, illustrator, and owner of Chickie & Roo, an educational curriculum and resource company for families and schools. She home educates her two children in Florida and taught in her local homeschool co-op community, where she led nature classes. Lauren is passionate about bringing children closer to nature and helping them develop a deeper understanding of our natural world. Her work has been featured in The Peaceful Press, A Year of Learning, Chickadees Wooden Toys, Wild + Free Co., FunSchooling Books, and more. You can find her work at chickieandroo.com.

STEPHANIE HATHAWAY is a Kansas City–area artist who specializes in creating educational content inspired by our natural world. She believes in using beautiful, dynamic illustrations to make learning about science and nature exciting and accessible to children of all ages. She is guided by the notion that many of life's valuable lessons can be learned from nature. It is her hope that her work will inspire families to explore and learn from the natural world right outside their own door. You can see more of Stephanie's educational nature-based studies and original artwork at stephaniehathawaydesigns.com.

LAURA STROUP is the founder of Firefly Nature School, a nature study curriculum designed for homeschooling families, co-ops, and classrooms found online at fireflynatureschool.com. Laura has a Bachelor of Science degree in Animal Ecology from Iowa State University with an emphasis in natural resource education. A former museum educator and upper school science teacher, she now directs School of the Wild, an immersive nature school that serves her local community. Laura resides in the countryside near Springfield, Missouri, with her family.

Quarto.com

© 2024 Quarto Publishing Group USA Inc.
Text, Illustrations © 2024 Lauren Giordano, Stephanie Hathaway, Laura Stroup

First Published in 2024 by Quarry Books, an imprint of The Quarto Group,
100 Cummings Center, Suite 265-D, Beverly, MA 01915, USA.
T (978) 282-9590 F (978) 283-2742

All rights reserved. No part of this book may be reproduced in any form without written permission of the copyright owners. All images in this book have been reproduced with the knowledge and prior consent of the artists concerned, and no responsibility is accepted by producer, publisher, or printer for any infringement of copyright or otherwise, arising from the contents of this publication. Every effort has been made to ensure that credits accurately comply with information supplied. We apologize for any inaccuracies that may have occurred and will resolve inaccurate or missing information in a subsequent reprinting of the book.

Quarry Books titles are also available at discount for retail, wholesale, promotional, and bulk purchase. For details, contact the Special Sales Manager by email at specialsales@quarto.com or by mail at The Quarto Group, Attn: Special Sales Manager, 100 Cummings Center, Suite 265-D, Beverly, MA 01915, USA.

10 9 8 7 6 5 4 3 2 1

ISBN: 978-0-7603-9194-5

Design and Page Layout: Mattie Wells
Illustration: Lauren Giordano, Stephanie Hathaway, Laura Stroup

Printed in China

MIX
Paper | Supporting responsible forestry
FSC® C016973
www.fsc.org

DEDICATION

This book is dedicated to children, families, and nature lovers everywhere. May you always explore with an open heart and open eyes.

CHECK OUT THE FULL SERIES

Nature School
978-0-7603-7835-9

Nature School: Planet Earth
978-0-7603-9197-6

Nature School: Planet Earth: The Workbook
978-0-7603-9199-0